If you find this book he
please write a review on Amazon.

Copyright © 2019 by Rich Reynolds
ISBN 9781074356163

ALL RIGHTS RESERVED, INCLUDING THE RIGHT OF REPRODUCTION
IN WHOLE OR IN PART IN ANY FORM.

Manufactured in the United States Of America.

Book authored and designed by Rich Reynolds

A special thanks to my friend and mentor BJW who provided all
the artwork and illustrations drawn and incorporated herein.

A sincere appreciation to my current and (hopefully) last wife LNG.

A Reynolds Media Publication

HOW TO WIN HER BACK
and not die trying!

......A MAN TO MAN CONVERSATION

By Rich Reynolds

TABLE OF CONTENTS

PREFACE..5

DISCLAIMER..8

PART ONE – TEN REASONS WOMEN OPT TO SEPARATE..9
1. SHE CAUGHT YOU CHEATING....NOW WHAT?............13
2. FALSE SENSE OF SECURITY..15
3. YOU ARE DEFINITELY FROM DIFFERENTPLANETS.......17
4. BOREDOM,....YOU JUST DON'TINTEREST HER ANYMORE!...20
5. LACK OF SUFFICIENT COMMUNICATION....................22
6. FEMALE SEXUALITY, HORMONES AND MID LIFE CHANGES..24
7. WOMEN FALL OUT OF LOVE QUICKER THAN MEN.....26
8. FEMALE INFIDELITY,...UNFORTUNATE BUT SOMETIMES PREDICTABLE..48
9. PEER PRESSURE AND MARRIAGE COUNSELING CAN GO EITHER WAY...51

10. "THE GRASS IS GREENER" SYNDROME........................54

CONCLUSION TO PART ONE..56

PART TWO – THE SECRET PLAN FOR WINNING HER BACK..61
STEP 1 - NO UNNECESSARY COMMUNICATION OR ENABLING..66
- WHAT ABOUT MONEY, FINANCIAL OBLIGATIONS & SETTLEMENT?...75
- WHAT ABOUT MY KIDS?..78
- STEP 1 SUMMARY AND REVIEW................................85

STEP 2 - OVERCOME YOUR LOSS...87
- HEAL AND MAKE YOURSELF WHOLE AGAIN..........92
- DATING TIPS..95

STEP 3 - TIME TO TAKE PROPER 'STOCK'.........................103
- MAKE YOURSELF MORE APPEALING WITH A PHYSICAL MAKEOVER...109
- WILL I 'LOSE' MY EX WHILE I'M GETTING MY ACT IN GEAR?...117
- WHAT CAN I EXPECT IF I'M THE ONE WHO WAS CHEATING,...AND GOT CAUGHT?.........................122

STEP 4 - TIME TO TEST THE *WATERS*................................124
- IT'S TIME TO *DIRECTLY* ASK YOUR EX TO MEET......135
- SHE SAID YES TO MEETING ME..............................137

WHAT TO DO IF YOU CHEATED...147

BRIEF SUMMARY OF THE ROAD TO WINNING HER BACK...153

SO, CAN I EXPECT TO MOVE BACK IN TOGETHER TOMORROW? 155

MAYBE YOUR MARRIAGE REALLY IS OVER OR SHOULD NEVER HAVE BEGUN! 159

QUIZ - DO I REALLY WANT TO GET BACK TOGETHER WITH MY EX? 161

CONCLUSION - BE CAREFUL WHAT YOU WISH FOR! 169

SO, YOU'VE BEEN THROWN OUT,
AND YOU WANT TO KNOW...

HOW TO WIN HER BACK
and not die trying!

...A MAN TO MAN CONVERSATION

By Rich Reynolds

PREFACE

First and foremost let me acknowledge that you are undoubtedly at an incredible low point in your life. You have been *dumped* by your wife, completely unnerved and almost panic stricken. More than likely you are consumed with thoughts regarding how to undo what has transpired. Possibly she simply left (with or without advising you in advance) or possibly you were *thrown out* of the matrimonial home. Either way, it was an abrupt, almost unsavory event leaving you devastated by the fact that your wife no longer loves you. Sleeping, working and normal day to day activities have become near impossible to perform. You are effectively paralyzed and all you keep thinking about is how to get your wife back. The strain is excessive, your stress level is extremely elevated and you have far more questions than answers. Suffice to say that your plight has been shared by millions and millions of men before you and almost all get through to the *other side* in one piece! And, while it might not be much consolation right now, your life is not over and things will definitely improve. You can be happy again and relatively soon.

In a nut shell, I gather that you want to find out how to get your ex-wife back and are wondering if this book can help? That's probably what's going through your mind as you read this,....."RIGHT?" You want to know (now) that, if you read this book and follow the suggestions closely,...can you win your ex-wife or girlfriend back. Or, is this book just another artsy, fartsy collection of rambling thoughts that some egotistical writer is using to make money,...at YOUR expense? Well, the short answer is YES, there is a good chance that you can win your ex back if you make the necessary changes and follow the "yellow brick road" (AKA the steps outlined herein). **I did**! BUT,......be careful what you wish for!

So, if your primary objective is to *induce* your wife to, once again, fall in love (with you) and hopefully reunite thereafter, you need to return to "functioning" status as soon as possible. You must get beyond the initial shock and begin rebuilding your composure and life immediately. The trauma is real and will take time to process. But, the healing aspect must begin as soon as realistically possible.

It might be beneficial to know that couples go through many phases during the course of their marriage. Life and responsibilities place huge demands and pressures on all of us and the consequences affect our general state of mind and our relationship with others. At times therefore, couples become more distant from one another. For certain periods they might even evolve in completely different directions. And, through the course of a marriage, couples frequently experience greater and lesser degrees of love for one another. In fact, it is not uncommon for one spouse to fall largely out of love with the other at some point during a *normal* marriage, particularly a long one. So, initially and in addition to becoming *whole* again, you'll want to focus on what went wrong in your marriage. You'll need to establish where things really got off the rails and how you were instrumental and/or responsible for that happening. And, you'll need to identify the changes that *you* are prepared to make? Egos and self-absorption will need to be put aside! Only in this way will there be a realistic chance of fixing the problems and hopefully reconciling the marriage. This book is definitely **not** a *pile of crap* and does contain the steps you'll need to win her back. But, your goal does require sincere reflection and a genuine effort.

Oh, one last thing. You will find a certain redundancy in many parts of this book; not because I have dementia and don't know when I'm repeating something,...but, because most men (including myself) are more akin to being 'block heads' than well-oiled machines! In other words, we need to be told things more than once and while we think that we generally know better,....we rarely do!

DISCLAIMER

Before I begin, I have three important messages and the point size should tell you something about the emphasis;

- **If you are a wife abuser, drug addict, alcoholic, some convoluted mixture of the aforementioned or some other equally mal-adjusted individual with personality disorders, your next step should NOT be to read this book, but rather to seek proper professional help as there's nothing in this book that will solve your personal or marital issues.**

- At the end of the proverbial day, the writings are based upon a collection of generalizations which are candidly and primarily derived from one opinion only,....mine! I believe that the book fairs well in describing, analyzing and predicting certain events as well as providing workable options for reversing a break-up. However, every situation is unique, every person is different and neither advice, strategy nor any book will ever cover all break-up and make-up possibilities, detail every character or contain resolutions to every problem and issue. This book is no exception and as your particular circumstances are unique to you, it is intended to serve as a possible guideline only. In fact, although this book is quite comprehensive, there is a chance that it does not cover your exact situation and specific characters which means that you will have to *cherry pick* whatever you deem to be meaningful and appropriate for your situation.

- In spite of multiple legal references contained herein, this book is not intended to provide legal advice in any way, shape or form whatsoever. However, it does suggest that you seek proper legal advice from a qualified and licensed solicitor in your area. Do yourself a favor and do so (in confidence).

PART ONE - TEN REASONS WOMEN OPT TO SEPARATE

OK,...let's get to it. On second thought, I strongly urge you to go back to the PREFACE and DISCLAIMER, which, if you are like a lot of other fellows (AKA,...me), you so hastily skipped. Please read it as it contains valuable information! Keep in mind that not one of us earthly humans is *all knowing* and/or *all seeing*. "Go slowly and you will not trip!"

So, I understand that you want to win your significant other back and will do just about anything it takes to do so. Suffice to say that it is quite doable and has been accomplished in many, many cases similar to yours. But, it is a process that will take time and possibly, considerable time. What makes me such an *authority*?.....well, intimate relations with several hundred women, four marriages, a multitude of male friends with failed relationships and a 20 year stint designing and manufacturing female *products*. In the course of the latter, I became somewhat of an expert/celebrity in the areas of female sexology, women's needs and corresponding marital characteristics. So, without sounding too arrogant, what I'm about to tell you is, in my opinion, fairly gospel. In fact, most of the information is common sense and/or text-book basic human nature. So, it can be actually relied upon to predict not every action that a woman takes,...but, many of them! In addition, this book delves into the basic reasons that women opt for separation as well as the multitude of marital mistakes that so many of my male brethren make.

Before I proceed further, I should caution you. It may sound odd or may even be purpose defeating,......but, the well-known adage that says "be careful what you wish for" might be worth mentioning here (again). The reality is that you may well move on in life before your ex even considers coming back. What's more, I'll advise you (as part of the *winning her back* process) to take forward moving steps (without her) for a variety of reasons. First and foremost, moving on will assist in your recovery, provide diversion and impart some sense of self-preservation all at the same time! For example, it's hard to be preoccupied with negative thoughts (about your ex) if you are getting ready for a date with someone new! Plus, human nature has shown us time and time again, that we always seem to want that which appears unattainable and/or even forbidden! In short, you are going to become ever so desirable when your ex knows that you are dating,...or *worse*...finds out that you have a new girlfriend. So, you might well have a rather tough decision to make downstream. I did! Additionally, I cannot emphasize enough that you need and should seek full and proper legal counsel NOW. You will undoubtedly find it a possibly unfixable but definitely (more) costly error should you fail to do so. If you consider the door to reconciliation as an open and viable possibility, keep your legal solicitations confidential and avoid an additional reason for confrontation with your ex.

At any rate, let me start at an appropriate beginning. It is paramount that you understand why your wife or partner left and/or gave you *walking papers*. Her reasons were likely verbalized or otherwise demonstrated on many occasions and were, to some lesser extent, as visibly *text-book* as ever. Candidly, in the absence of more serious reasons for leaving a marriage, like physical abuse or other criminal activity, alcoholism or gross irresponsibility, the vast majority of women who opt to leave their marriages, do so for a number of very predictable reasons. In fact, commonly there are several seemingly distinct but actually inter-related reasons that they opt to separate from their spouses. Accordingly, if you are fortunate enough to rekindle your relationship, make sure that you understand the reasons behind her departure in the first place and are prepared to address them with credible resolutions and alternative actions. You certainly don't want the same thing to happen again (and for the same reasons) further down the road!

There are effectively ten simple but consequential reasons that most women opt to separate. And rarely is there a solitary reason that has the wherewithal to single handedly end a marriage. It is usually three, four or more of these reasons, acting together, that tend to push our spouses over the proverbial edge. While certain women are pre-dispositioned to be affected more by one or another reason, it is unlikely that your spouse suggested separation for any substantive reason other than those detailed below. I have written a brief chapter on each of the ten basic reasons behind the vast majority of marital breakdowns. To give you an idea of what's ahead, I've summarized them below;

1) She caught you cheating,...or you were dumb enough to confess!

2) Your wife had a false sense of security created by *her* career, or *your* career, or other benefits / comforts attained through the marriage.

3) The two of you are from different planets and, as such have fundamentally different mindsets and needs.

4) Boredom and/or the realization that your ex-wife married beneath her 'bar.'

5) She realized that the lack of communication in your marriage significantly contributed to the deprivation of her basic marital needs.

6) She became symptomatic of out of control hormones (which can be disruptive to the lives of women and marriages).

7) During the *grinds* of marriage and over time, either spouse might well fall *out of love*. However, women tend to fall *out of love* quicker and more readily than men. What's more, they act upon it more readily as well!

8) Female infidelity is no longer an unusual event. In fact, many women are captivated by the euphoria of a fling wherein

enough might not be enough!

9) Peer pressure and professional advice doesn't always lead (us) in the right (or best) direction. And, sometimes, those *well-meaning* friends around us provide advice that is more self-serving (to them) than genuine.

10) She succumbed to the "grass is greener" syndrome. Some women believe that life in a neighbor's back yard is better than theirs!

Ten Reasons Women Opt to Separate

1) SHE CAUGHT YOU CHEATING....NOW WHAT?

She caught you cheating,...or you were dumb enough to confess. Infidelity is one of the most invasive acts that a husband can perpetrate on his spouse. You lied, you cheated and now she has *no* reason to continue trusting you. Suddenly, she feels utterly devastated. Where there was once a relative peaceful union of two people, there is now a big *divide* reminiscent of a deep and dark canyon where nobody is crossing to the other side. She has good reason to give you *walking papers* (if she hasn't already). Your actions represent a huge breach of trust and she is understandably and deeply hurt. An affair is arguably the most devastating single act that can be perpetrated against a spouse and marriage as it throws all credibility *out of the window* and garners a complete loss of faith in the guilty party.

Sometimes cheating men feel that they have good reason to cheat and occasionally, that may well be the case. Cheating husbands often recount that their home life has become loveless and intolerable and/or that their wife is no longer interested in sex. However, the ultimate affair is still an act of betrayal. Plus, there are other transgressions that are paramount to infidelity even though they might not be consummated by sexual intercourse. For example, a non-sexual extramarital relationship that includes social activities, personal confidences and other forms of physical contact still qualifies as being unfaithful. Clearly, it doesn't change the inherent truth that you committed a massive breach of trust and in so doing, undermined one of the most fundamental elements of the institution of marriage.

It is almost as if you've died and your wife is experiencing the sorrow of her loss. A massive *vacancy* has been opened in her life. The size of the wound is cavernous and the resulting pain is excruciating. Consider, for a moment, your feelings if the situation were reversed and your wife was the one cheating. I expect that you would be devastated and I doubt that *you* would be able to accept or acknowledge much, if any, explanation or justification.

However, time *does* heal most things and if you have other redeemable qualities, the marriage may not be over! When somebody cheats on a spouse, there is a pretty good likelihood that there are other problems inside the marriage. And, as the book's title suggests, it is possible to win her back if you identify those marital issues and address them. Even if you presently think that all is lost and there is no hope of (your ex) getting beyond your infidelity, I suggest otherwise. In fact, it is possible to move from infidelity to marital bliss. Marriages of more than two out of three couples survive a cheating spouse! With time, much reflection and considerable effort, your marriage can be repaired, improved and *made* stronger than before. On that basis and as I cover this topic again later in the book, I suggest that you keep reading and follow the guidelines herein.

2) **FALSE SENSE OF SECURITY**

Human nature has always led us to believe that marriage automatically provides a certain measure of security to each of its members. And while that might be the case in the early years, the opposite can easily become more prevalent later on. In fact, some married women tend to have a significant sense of false security following normal monetary successes that occur during marriages. This sense of false security is heightened if the husband is the significantly higher and primary income earner. Moreover, many men (like myself) go to great lengths to financially provide as much as we can to *please* our wives and create a stable family environment,….thinking that this will go a very long way in solidifying the marriage itself! Unfortunately, it doesn't necessarily accomplish what we want or expect! And women often overlook and seemingly disregard all the tangible assets that are built up during a marriage irrespective of who the primary earner was! Often they will delude themselves into thinking that the (wealth and comfort) status quo will continue after a separation. Commonly, they regard the disposable family (joint) income, their ability to purchase somewhat independently, the safety of the matrimonial house and other personal freedoms,...as *ground zero*. In other words, they tend to take it all for granted because they already have those things and presume that they will remain in place after a break-up. Sometimes, such misguided thoughts continue to prevail until after separation when the inevitable reality sets in that there **are** financial *consequences* from separating! In fact, some women can be caught completely *off guard* in these respects.

When my third wife opted out of the marriage, she was ultimately awarded almost $ 500,000, which was provided (in cash and by way of a new place to live). But, because of the standard of living that she was used to and which I created during our marriage, it was not enough and she burned through every dime, losing her new house in a few short years. It did not occur to her that she might have to maintain steady employment after the separation! Another one of my wives' was so expectant of all the wonderful things that I provided during the marriage, that, when she opted to leave, she was adamant that I had a secret hidden fortune (in an offshore bank account) that would fund her forever. She sued me. I spent $ 50,000 in legal bills and after a year of legal wrangling to locate the *hidden* accounts and funds that did not exist; she was awarded one quarter of the sum that I had originally offered her (before the court proceedings and legal wrangling even began)!

3) **YOU ARE DEFINITELY FROM DIFFERENT PLANETS**

While much argument exists today as to the extent of differences between the sexes, few dispute that each of the two spouses in a relationship functions on a completely different plain. A relative few number of things can bring a man and woman together in a relationship. A broad delineation would include infatuation, timing, sex, orchestration, attraction, flirtation, desire, insecurity and chance. But, there are an infinite number of beliefs, characteristics and predispositions that separate individuals, any one of which can ultimately drive a couple apart. Life philosophies, personal inequities, emotional maturity levels, sexual preferences, cultural backgrounds, ethnic upbringing, religion, politics, parents and general principles in and of themselves each provide enough capacity to create thousands of differences between spouses. In addition, everyone sees even the *same* things differently. Plus, everyone has different capacities for patience and stress. And, everyone has different moral fiber and tolerance levels.

In terms of relationships, men and women probably have quite varied perspectives on how they show their love and how they might appreciate being loved. To be clear, it would be rather unlikely if ten typical men could agree on the ways they prefer to receive love from their wives. One might think that the best way is through the allowance of frequent sex! Another might think that the best way is through platitudes and compliments. Similarly, ten average women would show similar disparity when comparing their preferred ways of receiving love from their husbands! So, when you put the sexes together in a relationship it stands to reason that major differences will not only exist, but they could easily be fundamental and profound which, of course, could then lead to stress, frustration and unhappiness.

Everyone has heard of or read the book "Men Are From Mars And, Women Are From Venus" written by John Gray (1992). The book suggests that there are inherent and intrinsic psychological differences between the sexes. The author sees men as cave-dwellers who *hunt and protect* and in so doing want to have these abilities recognized and appreciated. He categorizes women on the other hand as the communicators who strive to have their feelings understood and valued. Mr. Gray advances the notion that men really don't rate feelings very highly seeing them as being analogous with weakness and instability. He advances the theory further by stating that women don't generally appreciate these *abilities* of men. In Gray's view, women frequently regard men as aggressive and competitive with a general cold disposition. While John Gray serves up a multitude of means and mechanisms to bridge these apparent gaps between the sexes, there is little question that he sees men and women as originating from completely different planets!

The book "5 Love Languages" written by Dr. Gary Chapman (1995) arguably goes even further as he explains the disparity between the sexes. He states that men and women speak completely different languages when it comes to showing their love. Similarly he espouses how each sex might prefer receiving admonishment differently as well. He suggests that there are five separate "love languages" wherein some spouses like to receive love through one language while another prefers to receive love using an alternate language. For example, a woman might feel most loved when her husband spends quality time with her. A husband might feel most loved when his wife performs certain acts of service like allowing an extra *boys night*.

The bottom line is that there is great potential for distinction and diversity between the sexes on every conceivable level and to a multitude of degrees. Therefore, considerable work and effort are constantly required to minimize the negative effects of even the most superficial dissimilarities. Moreover, spousal differences are rarely benefited by time. If left unchecked, the quantity of marital differences and the severity will have huge impacts on the individuals and the marriage. Once differences of consequence gain a foot-hold tensions mount, frustration leads to unhappiness and anguish sets in. It is not long afterwards that a spouse might want out!

Did you spend sufficient time (during your marriage) ensuring that your *planets* were reasonably aligned?

4) BOREDOM,....YOU JUST DON'T INTEREST HER ANYMORE!

Boredom, often combined with the feeling that they have *outgrown* their male partners, is another key reason that women might leave seemingly stable relationships and/or marriages. The best of marriages go through cycles and many languish for long periods at status quo, mundane and/or *ho-hum* levels. And it seems to occur almost without anyone noticing. Children, jobs, finances and other *life* responsibilities all take a huge toll on the institution of marriage. It is commonly accepted that a relationship requires constant, concerted and joint efforts to keep it interesting and ensure that it continues to thrive. It takes time as well, something that many adults tend to have less and less of as life marches forward.

Marital boredom is felt by both husbands and wives. However, and interestingly, women generally notice and become influenced by the boredom issue first. To complicate the apparent *dreariness* of their mindset, women perceive their boredom and/or dissatisfaction from the lens of where they are in life at that moment (often after years of marriage) sometimes allowing little appreciation for the importance of the things that the union did "accomplish" or produce. In addition, car-pooling the kids to school, work/careers, after school children's activities, social activities, preparing meals and housekeeping all eat into the same 24 hour day, leaving little time to devote to the couple themselves!

So, while both men and women are chasing their careers, raising kids and administering the household, their marriage is effectively and almost always relegated to *second fiddle*. Most men seem to be able to contend with that *problem* while most women cannot! Inevitably and in order to escape the tedious routine and boredom, wives look beyond. Sometimes, that leads to counseling,....sometimes it leads to infidelity (see Chapter on Female Infidelity). But, more often it stirs up an entire spectrum of other marital issues! Either way, it might have been averted if I and many of my (guilty) male counterparts had simply put a tad more effort into sustaining the union. Arranging an occasional date night and/or bringing home flowers (when there isn't a formal occasion) are relatively inexpensive and easy ways to offset feelings of spousal boredom. They are not exclusively *fool-proof* solutions for sure,...but, in hind sight, they would have been painfully easy to undertake and undoubtedly helpful in my situations!

Some women are *preconditioned* to marry the football *jock*, firefighter, policeman, military or other stereotyped and *uniformed* man. And, it's frequently the uniform itself that emanates the attraction and not the man nor his character underneath. In these cases, the ladies are so enthralled by their *catch* that they initially gloss over the real substance of the man they married. As time passes, that substance frequently proves to be somewhat underwhelming and correspondingly disenchanting. So, as a word of caution to my friends in uniform,....make sure that you have something consequential *hidden* underneath that sexy ensemble,...and I don't mean below the waste!

Finally, some women realize (too late) that they might have married a guy that is just plain below their *bar*. Such men can often be characterized as the game and sports nut type,...in many cases, guys that simply refuse to grow up. These men love their video games and computer games and they can't live without their beloved NFL, baseball, basketball and hockey. I'm sure that you're getting the point. It is quite commendable that you might know the names and stats of every baseball player known to man! However, I don't really think that your ex gave a dam! She was/is undoubtedly looking for much more. Worse, a lot of these guys just don't cut it on the career front either and that's just plain double jeopardy for sure. Guys who manage to simultaneously fall into both of these categories really need to *get a life*. Indeed, they probably have to make some serious life altering decisions or they will remain permanently stagnant wherein few women will be interested on a long term basis.

5) LACK OF SUFFICIENT COMMUNICATION

A very common and legitimate complaint that married women have is that men stop *communicating* with them. It can be evident after merely a few short years or even a few brief months into the relationship. While one or both adults are preoccupied effectively outside the marital relationship with work, children and other responsibilities, women tend to feel the emotional disconnect first and most profoundly. As the result, they are often the ones to express it. I can't count the number of women that have said (to me) that "My husband and I just don't talk anymore!" In reality, this phenomenon is more a function of today's busy adults being simply too tired (to communicate), rather than any individual mal-intent or disrespect! Let's face it; we cover a lot of territory in one day. We work long hours, then come home and deliver the kids to after school activities. Then we prepare dinner, do a few chores, help the kids with their homework and then get them ready for bed. By the time we have 20 spare minutes for the spousal relationship, we're ready for bed ourselves! Clearly, these daily functions require a lot of time, effort and dedication, leaving little energy for much else. Nonetheless, those responsibilities inadvertently result in a reduction of communication (between spousal partners) and an unhealthy environment for a marriage. Moreover, lack of communication seems to take a larger toll on women.

In fact, for many men, simple silence and solace are (exactly) what they desire most after a typical work day,...whereas most women prefer quite the opposite. Women want to tell their husbands all about the things that happened in their day and they expect their partners to respond in kind. Sadly, many men frequently lack the patience to listen intently after a hard day's work! Plus, they typically don't want to relive the stresses of their own day by regurgitating every seemingly *painful* detail! As the result, many women yearn for the days of 'dating' when their men **did** communicate. Over time, many men climb further into their comfortable "cones of silence" while their wives become less interested in the relationship altogether! And ultimately (and frequently) this feeling of emotional detachment festers into a whole host of other marriage destroying scenarios.

Let's face it, if the basis for your wife's perception of a solid relationship is regular emotional support garnered through spousal communication and it is lacking, why would she need the spouse at all? From this simple perspective, she would be in the same emotional place without the spouse and without the relationship! Once again gentlemen, while everyone is tired after a long day's work, it doesn't really take much (additional) effort to open a sincere twenty minute dialogue with your significant other! Silence is definitely **NOT** golden in a relationship.

6) FEMALE SEXUALITY, HORMONES AND MID LIFE CHANGES

The North American Menopause Society (NAMS) says this about female sexuality,

*"If you had to choose one word to describe women's sexual function and sexual health, you'd be wise to go with the word **complex**. The factors that contribute to women's sexual health and satisfaction, as well as their sexual problems, are many and often interrelated. These factors range from physical changes of menopause and aging to a woman's physical health, her cultural and religious standards, issues in her relationship, her self-image and stress and lifestyle issues."*

For many women in their 40's and 50's, hormones and the *change in life* are unwitting but significant factors in their decision to leave a marriage. With menopause, it is not uncommon for women to refocus their direction on what **they** want from life. In addition, and while menopause is normal and happens to all women, some of the symptoms can be frustrating, upsetting, painful, destabilizing and even destructive. So, much so, in fact, that menopause in middle aged women can be a primary terminating force on a marriage! Hot flashes, decreased libido, insomnia, general irritability, mood changes and even depression are common symptoms (although in varying degrees within and amongst each individual). Commonly, a woman's needs and desires for spousal relations drops off significantly during this period and sometimes lasts indefinitely. Changing hormones brought on by middle age can increase the *average* emotional swings dramatically in both severity and frequency and can completely alter the normal thought process as well as the means by which major decisions are made. It is no strange coincidence that women, in their menopause years (40 to 60), are responsible for initiating three quarters of the marriage separations in the western world.

In some cases, mid-life changes and increased testosterone have brought a dramatic *increase* in a woman's libido while still introducing, many of the other more common symptoms to a person's newly altered life. In those situations the woman will want much more sex than was the previous norm, and often more than her husband can provide! This can be equally unsettling and destabilizing. I am personally aware of several (otherwise stable) marriages that broke up (after lengthy periods) due to the wife's increased libido!

For many years, physicians prescribed long term use of an oral estrogen/progesterone combination to alleviate some of these symptoms. However, *turn of the century* studies found that long term use of hormone replacement drugs resulted in higher risks of stroke, cardiovascular disease and breast cancer. My own (current) mother-in-law contracted cancer in this way. As the result, current enlightened physicians will recommend temporary hormone replacement therapy for only cases with more extreme symptoms. For more average needs they opt for safer, but less effective remedies, like non-hormonal medications (for very specific symptoms), topical estrogen creams (for vaginal lubrication) and promote improvements in diet, fitness and stress relieving activities.

Suffice to say that there is no easy way for either the woman suffering with the results of hormonal changes, or her significant other, to transgress beyond this often difficult period. Most marriages are made up of mere mortals and as such, both spouses take an awful toll. Husbands do not always provide the necessary emotional support during these vulnerable times and wives often make rash decisions that can manifest into unfortunate marital demise.

7) **WOMEN FALL OUT OF LOVE QUICKER THAN MEN**

You have already read many explanations as to why women might opt to leave their marriages. So, it goes without saying that those same potential relationship terminators are similarly responsible for why women fall out of love (which, of course, is usually the precursor to a separation) in the first place. But, there are a multitude of other reasons as to why women fall out of love and I have listed the ten most common below.

THE EMOTIONAL SPARK IS GONE - *Sparks* are common in the courting and falling in love stages of a relationship for both men and women. In reality, the spark is an essential necessity for going from the early casual dating phase to the latter more dedicated boyfriend/girlfriend (being in love) stage. They are symptomatic of euphoric, tingly feelings not readily generated in any other way. Unfortunately, the spark often tends to wither once the relationship has moved into the more permanent stage. The dating excitement gives way to regular relationship and marital routines and a certain degree of *feeling* is lost. In essence, the relationship tends to get ordinary and even stale and if both individuals do not put in a quantifiable effort, they will find themselves in a rut very quickly. Women tend to be bothered by this loss of spark more-so than men. However, men can do so much to appease them! Should you get another opportunity at a relationship with your ex-spouse, I strongly urge you to make every effort to introduce and maintain more sparkling nuances into your revived marriage than you did before. Try (periodically) arranging a romantic dinner for two at her favorite restaurant, purchasing a piece of lingerie, bringing home chocolates, visiting your local adult store together or surprising her with a candle lit massage and bath. These will go a long way in rejuvenating and preserving the spark!

REOCCURRING ISSUES - One of the most appealing yet divisive characteristics in relationships is the simple fact that **no** two people are alike. In regards to husbands and wives, the degree of dissimilarity can range dramatically. The unknown, the excitement and the mystery that accompanies meeting another person can be very appealing. There is no question that in many, many cases opposites do attract. It is not uncommon that women like *bad boys* and men in uniform while men are more apt to let certain appendages choose their dates! Several of my short term relationships and two of my failed marriages were the direct result of my reproductive organ choosing my direction! I semi-seriously refer to *him* as my "Mini Me." Nonetheless, it is of no surprise that, with these seemingly *desirable* diversities, come completely different views on many important marital topics. Even when two individuals feel that they are somewhat similar, they are, in fact, not so similar at all. Invariably they will have small to enormously different views on just about anything and everything including, child rearing, politics, finances, house cleaning, division of chores/labor, work ethics and careers. As time goes on, these varying views begin to surface more regularly and tend to be a source of irritation to one or both parties.

Then there is the whole list of tier two personal items that can also be a major source of frustration to one partner or the other. Things like unacceptable personal attire, lack of cleanliness, constant lateness/unreliability, irregular driving styles and polarized eating/drinking habits can certainly be a source of irritation. It only takes one unresolved recurring issue to initiate cracks in the union.
While it matters not who is the *nagger* and who is the *nag-gee*, women are generally more sensitive to these types of recurring relationship issues than men. Or, at minimum, women are more likely to react. With time a woman will feel that she is unable to bring about any meaningful change regarding the *problem*. The frustration will turn into resentment and ultimately cause serious damage to the relationship. So, guys, next time around, try to avoid some of the recurring problems by simply reducing the quantity of potential issues. Pick up your dirty clothes and put them in the hamper, reconsider your position on one of the contentious spousal view-points...and maybe help out with the vacuuming once in a

while!

COMPLACENCY ...THE SILENT MARRIAGE KILLER - It is quite possible that complacency ranks as the number one *sleeper* culprit capable of almost single handedly causing total marital breakdown. At minimum, this subtle demon will fuel the process of falling out of love and possible infidelity until there is little left in the union. The logic behind this is simple,.....life is onerous, time consuming and exhausting. Most of us have jobs, children, chores, pets and other responsibilities. Who amongst us mere mortals has additional energy for much else? Even those seemingly perfect, super-human adults, with endless energy, are prone to taking their spouses for granted. Our stories are all rather similar. We meet online, at a bar or in school; we become infatuated, fall in love and move in together. Before long we get married and then the inevitable happens,...life overwhelms us with its unexpected demands and complexities, our marriage takes second fiddle and we become complacent to it.

Many couples and particularly men believe that marital complacency is merely an insignificant lull or bump in the marriage cycle,....a phase that is simply temporary. As a consequence, they give the *state* little attention! But, marital complacency is serious, rarely resolves itself and requires effort and time to rectify. Unfortunately, wives often feel the lion's share of the consequences of a stagnating relationship more than their husbands. In fact, even when a marriage is knee deep in complacency, married men tend to avoid the efforts needed to prevent the marriage from slipping further into the abyss. If the pattern continues unabated, with the marriage wallowing in the doldrums, the end could well be near. But, it is an extremely avoidable outcome. A nominal amount of input by either partner to disrupt the routine is an easy start. It takes only a relative small, heart-felt effort to show your spouse that you still care; a hand touch, a few kind words or a simple flower speak volumes in these regards. Husbands frequently fail to tell their wives that they (still) love them, believing that it is understood and therefore unnecessary. They rarely initiate the effort to have regular "us" time and they seldom communicate with the sincerity and depth needed by most women. These are classic mistakes from which many marriages do not survive.

DWINDLING PASSION — Generally speaking, quality of sex is at its highest and best when it is the newest. Consequently, sex with the same person year after year tends to become rather ordinary as the novelty is gone and neither spouse puts in the same effort as before. For many men it becomes a classic *wham, bam, thank you mam* and for women it can end up being something that they just want to *get over with*. As a general rule, the longer that a marriage *survives*, the more that sexual quality and frequency will abate. Compounding this common scenario is young children not sleeping through the night, work stresses, exhaustion and other issues in the marriage. Women, in particular, inadvertently allow daily responsibilities and other marital frustrations to overshadow physical relations with their spouse. Preoccupation with a husband's bothersome habits, unresolved problems around money and a whole host of other marital issues will completely sideline a woman's psyche in bed. Men, on the other hand, tend to get lazy over time and circumvent all the things that warm women up to the occasion. Massages, mood setting candles, foreplay and special little techniques rarely see the inside of a bedroom after a few short years of marriage! Plus, sometimes there are outside influences that affect physical relations between couples. That cute flirtatious girl at the office and that hunky guy in the lunchroom add to the multitude of distractions and pressures already placed on marital intimacy. With normal stresses of the day, at any given moment, a husband or wife could easily cave to the charms of an admirer. While it might be too late for your current failed relationship (or at least round one), be cognizant for next time that it's important to communicate as to one another's needs, use imagination to keep the "bedroom" interesting and generally make real efforts to keep your marital sex relations alive and vibrant.

LYING - Total honesty is clearly the best policy! But, is it that simple? It certainly isn't always that easy. Telling your spouse absolutely everything can be incredibly comforting, at least in theory. However, are there not situations when the unbridled truth is hurtful to one side or the other? Take the overweight wife who is longing to be told how beautiful she (still) is! Most husbands will mimic those words without regard to the truth. Some people believe that telling little white lies is OK,...as long as they are relegated to the ones that might protect a person's feelings. So, you tell your wife that her hair looks great when, in fact, her new blue streak really doesn't look good at all. The philosophical problem with the acceptance of these little white lies is that when asked what the most important character trait in a spouse might be, most people say honesty! So, where is the line?

Marital counselors, psychologists and couples therapists alike will unanimously maintain that couples should always tell the truth to one another, no matter what! Unfortunately, they frequently spout lofty, euphoric justification that is hard to fully embrace. Reasons like holding back will ruin your relationship and failing to be completely honest prevents you both from moving forward. How about, "You'll be a better person and it will be easier to get through those rough times if you are totally forthcoming!" Will it really be easier? I can certainly envision circumstances when telling the truth could be far more difficult and damaging! Moreover, while these mission statements sound wonderful, they are rather lacking in real substance.

Nevertheless, and for the most part, it is hard to rationally argue in favor of any amount of common place lying particularly in a marriage. Honesty instills confidence, reduces stress, increases general trust of one another and absolutely strengthens relationships. So, at minimum, I would recommend that you should never lie to your spouse about your relationship needs, your feelings towards one another and the extent of love that you actually have for your spouse. Nor is it recommended that you lie about such things as your future plans, your desires in regards to sex, how you are feeling and doing, kids and generally, the *big ticket* items.

Yet, one of the most common items that both married individuals lie about is sex. Most likely the reason stems from the often misguided thinking that one person will hurt, annoy or upset the other if they are brutally honest and upfront. However, there is so much out there in the realm of experimentation, that most current generation adults would love to try something new to supplement their love life! So, raising a 'touchy' issue (like unsatisfying sex) and being honest about it might well have very beneficial results for both spouses. Certainly, when the topic is contentious or potentially hurtful, make sure that you use tact, tenderness and a gentle conveyance. Try to provide a positive delivery with meaningful and balanced suggestions instead of mere criticism. Maybe a trip to an adult toy store is in the offing or maybe an XXX movie (of her choice). Your spouse will undoubtedly like whatever you suggest particularly if it is fun, unique and outside your normal routine! Pretend that you are on the other side of the unwelcome news and be heartfelt during the discussion! But, remember too, that certain distasteful news can become a double edged sword! In other words, be ready to receive as well!

What about being completely honest when it comes to financial issues and third party attractions? Can the average woman really handle her husband telling her that he's got an insignificant crush on his 20 year old secretary? Will all women react in a perfectly balanced and supportive way to rumors that their husband's employer might be closing down? Does the added and arguably unnecessary stress placed upon her really have a positive or beneficial result? Many women might respond with a hundred different questions, tears and/or criticism. Would that not actually increase the stress on the husband and the marriage? What would happen if, due to that added stress, a husband were to overlook something critical and inadvertently cause a larger and otherwise avoidable (financial) problem?

These are not easy questions to answer. However, there is one fact that is an inescapable reality. When either spouse is caught lying on a topic of consequence (like cheating), the relationship will be seriously affected and the marriage significantly harmed. Neither spouse can readily handle the realization that they have been seriously deceived, nor see past it very easily. And, even if you volunteer the occurrence of infidelity (before being caught), the results are still likely be devastating (no matter how positive the delivery and remorseful you might be). Men have a lot of pride and often sizable issues with jealousy that can cloud an easy recovery from a deceitful wife. When it comes to a husband lying, women will have lengthy trust issues thereafter and hold grudges for some considerable time,....if not longer!

So, what is the ultimate answer when it comes to telling the truth,...or opting to lie? While I do not condone lying, I do appreciate that life, marriage and the unusual situations that comprise both make resolution analysis and implementation extremely complex. So much so that adhering blindly without question to hard and fast rules about truths is probably overly simplistic, difficult to carry out and possibly even counterproductive for certain sets of circumstances. For one thing, people are not robots and nobody reacts to difficult news in the psychologically perfect, balanced, common sense and supportive fashion that the therapists like to predict! So, the result of **every** honest gesture is hardly, much less, automatically moralistic and beneficial to both parties. In fact, I emphatically do understand how withholding certain pieces of distressing information (from one's spouse) might serve the better good in isolated situations. That story above about the husband withholding information about financial pressures,...well, that was me in one of my marriages. We were in the middle of a massive recession, under huge financial pressures and I chose not to enlighten my wife as to the entire seriousness of our situation. Had I filled her in entirely, her reactions (very likely compounded by her substance abuse) would have been so volcanic and toxic that the result would have given *me* a heart attack upon first disclosure!

Gentlemen, while the ultimate decision as to telling truths is your's, I do recommend careful thought, a thorough understanding of potential responses and the overall consideration of benefits/detriments associated with lying and/or withholding important information. However, with that in mind, I strongly urge you to stay well on the good side of honesty as much as realistically possible. If you are already separated, your tendency to be less than candid may well have contributed to the break-up. So, should you win her back or enter marriage number two with a new lady, remember that honesty and the marriage duration are directly related. In other words, if you are largely honest, your relationship will last longer!

THE HONEYMOON IS OVER - For many married men the *seven year itch* comes at around the three year mark! Married women tend to experience something a little different around that same time. Very simply they feel that the *honeymoon* is over,...and, it is for any one of a multitude of reasons! Here is a short, but commonly felt list of reasons why the honeymoon is, in fact, over!

- Some women (and men) have an unrealistic expectation as to what marriage will actually be about. In reality, it's clearly not an ongoing love-fest or party!

- Some spouses are unnerved by the addition of more responsibilities than they had before the union,...and in many circumstances double!

- Many adults actually have difficulty sharing space with another person who has different views on a lot of topics (like living arrangements, house cleaning, finances, cooking, etc.).

- Both sexes have been known to trade an undesirable home life (with parents) for an unknown married situation,....assuming that the latter will be an improvement.

- Some married individuals find out (the hard way) that their spouse's future goals and plans aren't quite aligned with theirs.

- Other married individuals find, after a few years of marriage, that their spouse is not as flexible (as they were hoping) on some critical items.

- Most married people find that the quality time spent together is much more infrequent and not at all like it was when they were dating.

- Many couples often feel that little things that were previously overshadowed by the euphoric dating process are now frustrating in the marriage.

- Both sexes frequently find themselves spending much **less** time thinking about their spouse than they did before the marriage.

- It is not beyond the realm of possibility that one spouse or the other, realizes that they fell in love for the wrong reasons (or to the wrong person).

- Within a few short years, both men and women tend to forget some of the reasons that they fell in love in the first place.

- With time and life's preoccupations and responsibilities, Women (in particular) often don't feel as adored as they did before getting married.

- Both sexes (but women more predominantly) tend to miss the euphoric dating and *falling in love* stage. Losing those feelings (forever) can be a difficult reality.

- Women (and men to a lesser extent) tend to miss the lengthy conversations & emotional connections that were more prevalent during the dating stage.

- Many couples find that they don't have the same shared purpose that they had when they were dating.

- While complete honesty is definitely in order for all marriages, doing and saying exactly what's on your mind now has greater consequences.

- Some spouses begin to neglect themselves after marrying. Their personal appearance changes as he or she doesn't take the same care as before.

- It is not unusual for one spouse or the other to feel tied down. They might even express the feeling,...as for example, "I used to be independent and now I feel exactly the opposite."

- It is not uncommon for couples to disagree more often than they might have during the dating stage. Consequently, marital arguments tend to be more frequent.

- Tension and stress that was rarely felt before, commonly sneaks into marriages.

And that is a short list of the realities facing newlyweds and longer term couples! While all of the above are common to both sexes, wives tend to take these feelings more to heart while men tend to get on with other facets of marriage and life (like their work and career). Also, these items are on the negative side of the equation. There is definitely a positive side and many ways to keep the honeymoon stage going (longer if not indefinitely) as well. For example, there is now someone with whom to share the ups and downs of life. There is a sense of security that comes from being part of a couple and you (theoretically) now have a built-in support structure for your personal endeavors.

While you might be already separated (or in the post honeymoon doldrums), there is a whole host of things that one can do (next time) to keep the honeymoon spirit alive. For example, try creating new endeavors that you can enjoy together like cooking classes or joining a wine tasting club. Spend some discovery time in the bedroom and find new and interesting ways to spice up your sex life. Husbands, in particular, should make time to continue providing many of the little nuances that made the honeymoon what it was,...like buying chocolates/flowers, kissing your wife unexpectedly, sending 'sweet nothing' texts and calling during the work day just because!

IT WAS NEVER REAL TO BEGIN WITH - If, in relative short order, your wife went from being starry-eyed, head-over-heels in love wanting almost endless physical contact to the realization that you and she lack chemistry, are emotionally disconnected and she is bored to tears,...then it is very possible that your wife was never truly in love in the first place. She simply had a fling (with you) and/or was otherwise misguided into thinking that it was more. It's not common that one goes from fling to marriage but it does happen and probably equally for both sexes. It occurs for any one (or more) of a number of reasons from immaturity regarding relationships to the age old rebound. Many women have been driven to marry a fling-mate by their desire for children and/or the pressure of their biological clock (ticking away). Many men are misguided by physical attractions and sex. And, even more women get so caught up in the Cinderella story, believing that everything will work out simply because "we love each other."

I realized that I had made a massive mistake on the first night of my actual second honeymoon. It was late at night, my bride was asleep in the passenger seat and we were driving to our hotel. The apparent solitude and tranquility of the night drive brought a multitude of thoughts to my mind,...the biggest one being, "What the hell did I just do?" I realized that I was definitely on the rebound. I had thought that I could help her with her issues and had allowed my "mini-me" (otherwise known as my penis) to lead me astray, yet again! It was probably the most monumental "Oh F_ _K" moment of my life,...and I've had my fair share of those! Clearly, I should have typed an excel spreadsheet detailing the pros and cons prior marrying this woman! It wasn't long before that oversite proved disastrous!

Both men and women are rather fickle beings. Our understanding of the word *love* is severely limited and naïve at best. We meet someone new, we exchange approving glances, someone says something nice, we feel a bit of euphoria and presto,...we're in love. How the heck is that even possible? At the early stages we generally know nothing about their true sense of being, little about their substance (other than the superficial appearances) and their quality of character has yet to be tested by life's trials and tribulations. What's more, their degrees of morality and ethics are nicely shrouded in the clouds of love. Yet, because we're *in love*, we tend to excuse, justify or otherwise explain away everything that we find not quite aligned with our gleeful emotions and expectations. And, we continue on blissfully.

Remember also, that our parents communicated absolutely nothing about the subject of love when we were growing up (stressing only that we should not get some young lady pregnant before marriage). We were taught zero in school and the vast majority of us never read a single book on the topic of love or relationships prior to marrying! So, it should come as no surprise that we are all pretty clueless in that regard and as such, society should be ecstatic that the divorce rate is not 100%.

MEN CAN BE SUCH SCREW-UPS – Being of the male persuasion myself, one would think that this is an easy topic to discuss. Yet, the simplicity is so counterintuitive! Men are quite capable of screwing up just about anything and everything when it comes to marriage and relationships. There are a huge number of basic marital screw-ups that we frequently make. But, before I *let loose* with an embarrassing list of those tid-bits, let me digress to an important topic for one brief moment.

There is one aspect of relationship learning that therapists and counselors rarely communicate and self-help books generally miss or ignore altogether. I briefly nudged the topic above under "It Was Never Real To Begin With." Very simply, few parties to a marital union (men or women), actually took the time to properly *take stock* at the outset,...in other words, before you say "I do!" As you may or may not be aware, we are in an extremely vulnerable mindset during the dating phase. Our judgement is clouded by personal insecurities, there are constant thoughts that we can't let this opportunity pass, we are confused and fearful (of failing) and we make completely baseless and misguided assumptions to satisfy peers. And then, of course, there are the physical aspects of a new relationship that skew our thinking in a novel way.

Yet, prior to taking the next step, few of us actually take the time to compose a simple spreadsheet of the pros and cons of marrying this particular person! It is not as ridiculous or crude as it might sound. Possibly a tad crass,...yet, incredibly useful! With a plus 50% divorce rate and two people involved in every break-up, think of all the pain, suffering and loss of years that might be avoided. Would it have been so difficult or unusual to create a simple list of positives, negatives and reasons (as to why this might be the best partner,...or not). Would it have been so *wrong* to provide an honest and credible review of such a list and then act upon the results? Probably not! Yet few of us have ever considered doing so.

Creating a simple functioning list (of pros and cons) need not even include more than 10 or 20 items. Simple questions like, does he want children, is she a *neat freak*, does he have realistic career goals, does she want to live in an urban environment or a farm field, is he a vegetarian, can she manage money, is he a control nut, does he snore,.....etc. Let's face it, after two or three months in a relationship most everyone is pretty transparent and the answers to your key needs and concerns will be terribly evident. But, that's a bit late and it would have been ever so useful to have reviewed a spreadsheet beforehand! I have been married four times and don't recall creating a list prior to marriage even once!

I think that the easiest way to demonstrate how unreasonable and counterproductive men can be in a relationship, is by providing **positive and constructive recommendations** that will be helpful should you win her back or in your next relationship. I am not suggesting that wives are *all perfect* and blameless in the breakdown of relationship harmony. But, this book does have the theme of **you** winning her back after a separation, so I will continue with the male perspective here!

- Try not to be an overbearing ass (all the time),...you need not commandeer every discussion and win every dispute with her. Frankly, nobody cares how smart you think you are and your wife will surely join those ranks in short order. So, try giving in to her views once in a while and see the positive results that will stem from that!

- Is it really so difficult to stop and buy flowers occasionally and for no reason other than to say "I love you?"

- Do something different and special for her on a semi-regular basis. Book a ski holiday or a three day cruise or arrange a simple weekend at a nice hotel once a year so that your spouse isn't bored to tears with the everyday marital responsibilities and YOU.

- Calm the hell down. Your name is not preceded by the word 'King.' Take a notch off and stop acting like you're better than everyone else. Your shit stinks and you are average and ordinary at best, so stop pretending otherwise. Life is stressful enough without the addition of your personal insecurities. You are not expected to be perfect and you are surely not perfect. So, act human!

- Mention some good things that your wife does and don't wait for an occasion. In other words, volunteer how grateful (and happy) you are with something that she does on a regular basis.

- Give your spouse some space to remain an individual. Don't you want the same?

- Text her a love note. Let her know that you really care.

- Kiss and snuggle at times **when you don't expect sex immediately thereafter.** I know,...that's a tough one!

- Pour her a nice (candle lit) bath.

- Give her a massage. You might even get lucky!

- Encourage her to continue seeking out her (solo) goals. You do not have a monopoly on goal setting/chasing. Be aware that many women who follow the 'stay at home mother' *dream*,...regret it years later. So, you'll regret it too!

- Talk to your wife more often and most of all,...LISTEN! But, also, after she has told you about her day,....tell her about yours. In spite of the frequent male tendency to just "bury" the day once you get home, try and find something that you might convey nonetheless.

- Be honest and don't lie,....at minimum with regards to the important things.

- Don't make her totally responsible for the health and wellbeing of the relationship.

- If YOU are responsible for any of the recurring issues and disagreements, try to come up with a solution or middle ground so that the recurrence comes to an end.

- Don't get complacent. If you feel or recognize the tendency, suggest a new shared experience that you can both try. Use your imagination to come up with shared activities that spice up the non-sex part of your marriage.

- Schedule a regular "date night" and try not to be late!

- Don't be habitually late (or absent) for dinner and/or family events.

- Try and remember that it's NOT all about you. Ask her how she's doing and/or how she's feeling from time to time.

- Try not to be a complete slob. Pick up your dirty clothes and put them in the hamper. Clear your beer cans and other mess from the coffee table after a game. Wash your own clothes occasionally and vacuum more than once a year! If you can operate your cell, you can figure out how the washing machine works!

- You are now officially an adult,...so, act like one and toast the video games. In other words, GROW UP! Above all, don't be a couch potato.

- Keep up your appearance. Moreover, if you look like a lot of today's dudes,...take steps to immediately improve your appearance,....a lot (because you look like a scruffy kid).

- She may not be into sports like you are. So, pass on the occasional Sunday football game. I am pretty sure that your world won't collapse.

- If you have chores,...DO THEM sooner rather than later. Let her know that you are reliable,...at least occasionally!

Well, it is becoming apparent that I am getting more upset, impatient and sarcastic as this already lengthy list (of men's marital failings) gets longer and longer. I'm sure that all you guys get the message by now and fortunately, there is a lot of guidance under Part 2 so that you have a real chance of reconciliation. But, should you get that opportunity, make sure that you (come back and read and) incorporate all the above into your life and new relationship.

On that note, I'll move onto another reason why women fall out of love with men.

MARRIED WOMEN OFTEN DON'T FEEL LOVED, ADORED AND NEEDED ANYMORE - Surprisingly (or maybe not) both men and women tend to process their general love needs in much the same way. Both require admiration, adoration, tenderness and appreciation especially at the beginning. However, most married men have a tendency to become engulfed in other things once the dating period and honeymoon are over and the novelty wears off. They generally become preoccupied with their career, finances and/or kids and don't really notice (initially) or miss the waning of regular complimentary reinforcements. Whereas married women need a constant fuel supply of emotional connectivity, psychological (and non-physical) intimacy and gratuitous appreciation no matter what career ambitions or family aspirations they might also have. Big words and scary terminology for sure! But, it all boils down to this. Married women need to know that their man still loves them and needs them, and there will likely never come a time in your marriage when they don't want to feel that. As women periodically gauge the quality of their marriage, they place a high emphasis on the emotional and loving vibes that you continue to provide....or don't!

So, if you are fortunate enough to get another opportunity to repair things with your ex or should you move on to a new relationship, make sure that you remember the following;

- It's not a simple matter of you actually loving your wife. She needs to *know* that you love her!

- Try not to be emotionally absent when you are together.

- On topics that are important to her, show your wife the degree of understanding that you might want to receive in the reverse situation.

- Treat her with the same respect that you expect! So, when she makes a mistake (think first about all the times you screwed up and), don't get carried away. Let it go because the constant criticism is hurtful and psychologically wearing. Plus, most mistakes really aren't life altering.

- Be affectionate to your wife and show some tenderness.

- When she raises something that is bothering her,...show some empathy, even if you think it's trivial; because it isn't trivial to her!

- Be kind and compassionate. Believe it or not, you can still be the macho tough guy too!

- By the way, most women don't want a pussy for a husband! They don't want a wimp or game playing child in a 42 regular. BUT, they don't want Rambo either. They want someone supportive and responsible who takes initiative but has regard for the opinion of others (namely, hers).

- When she does something for you, don't take it for granted. Let her know that you really appreciate it. Your wife wants to know (from you) that she's needed. Tell her that her helpfulness is one of the many reasons you married her. But, be prepared for her to ask what some of the other reasons were/are,.....and you had better have that list at your fingertips!

MANY WOMEN FEEL TOTALLY AND SOLELY RESPONSIBLE FOR ENSURING THE SUCCESS OF THE MARRIAGE AND THE RELATIONSHIP - Keeping a marriage healthy and a relationship strong, is a full-time job for TWO people and if your wife felt that it was all up to her,...well, that might be why she's gone! So, gents don't think that as you might have undertaken certain menial requirements of the marriage (like cutting the grass, taking care of car repairs and/or handling finances), that your wife automatically became more responsible for its general wellbeing! While chores are clearly a vital aspect of life,...they have little to do with the direct success of relationships. Marriage is not an entity to which the critical contributions and efforts can be made disproportionately or with a check book!

You both have to contribute, relatively equally and in most areas. So, either *suck* it up and "tow the line" or stay single the rest of your life. Your wife is not solely responsible for the success or failure of the marriage and all the related nuances. She is not totally responsible for child rearing. She is not totally responsible for the social aspects of your relationship. Quite simply, she is not totally responsible for anything! It is important for you to contribute as much as possible. In addition to your full-time employment, the following is the minimum that you should be undertaking for the wellbeing of the relationship;

- Frequently initiate conversations. It really doesn't have to be about anything in particular or it might be about something that is important. Just keep lines of communication open. For example, ask her what interesting things might be going on at work.

- Set up some of the outings (double-date) with friends and try and pick friends that she likes.

- Try and share picking up the kids from school. If you can't share the responsibility 50/50, make sure that you do it as frequently as possible and preferably on Fridays when you are also suggesting that she take a spa day!

- Contribute to keeping the *spark* alive by suggesting new sensual activities. You can actually make an *outing* of visiting your local adult store to buy something fun! Ask your wife what she might like to try!

- Offer to do the grocery shopping on a regular basis.

- Arrange regular *date* nights that involve something she likes to do (whether you like the activity or not)! Don't ever be the one to cancel.

- When your wife is feeling overwhelmed, ask how you can help and DO WHATEVER SHE SAYS.

- Do something special for your wife,.. something out of the ordinary that she wouldn't expect.

- Share the responsibility of child rearing 50/50 including, but not limited to, assisting with their homework and putting them to bed.

- Call your wife during the day and ask how she's feeling and is there anything that you can do for her.

So, if you are reading this book, chances are that you didn't provide a sufficient amount of the emotional support that your wife needed. Instead of facilitating more of the things that keep a marriage healthy,.....you were undoubtedly *MIA* and your wife grew to believe that she had the lion's share of responsibility for the marriage.

Trying to draw a positive conclusion to this chapter was difficult. Much of the content was/is, to be honest, rather scary! The section raised many male imperfections and failings while suggesting that women's needs are so onerous that they require huge efforts to *keep* them content and loving us! In fact, it appears that there is so much potential for women to fall *out of love*, that the odds are stacked against success from the outset. And, are men really completely responsible for our wives falling out of love?

In reality, the answer probably lies somewhere in the middle. But, clearly I'm not going to spend a lot of time or effort delineating all the flaws of the fairer sex because men are even more flawed and this book is aimed at them. The simple fact remains that these writings are primarily about *winning her back*. So, I will leave the female digressions to those with better perspective and appropriate qualifications.

Suffice to say however, that from the male disposition, our own insecurities, buried emotions and head strung desire to *beat to other drums* (AKA, intentionally avoid the obvious) are huge contributors to our spouses disenchantment and discontent. It surprises me little that they frequently fall out of love with us. Our own relationship insecurities make for a lengthy list and *challenge* much of the male sense of 'being' including our ability to attract women in the first place.

A man's psyche is constantly under *attack*. We fend off daily pressures regarding our career, our financial endeavors, our sexual abilities, our physical appearance, our capacity to cope and our ability to measure up to her expectations. Yet, instead of dealing with these insecurities *head-on*, we tend to cover them up often by redirecting them onto our spouse under the guise of her inadequacies! No wonder our wives so frequently fall out of love with us. I was 42 years old before I realized the wasted effort and counter productiveness of feeling jealous and stopped driving myself (and my spouse) *crazy*.

8) FEMALE INFIDELITY,... UNFORTUNATE BUT SOMETIMES PREDICTABLE

This is a topic that no married man wants to acknowledge as even being possible, unless, of course, we're on the other side! And, yes, I can hear you all saying that "My demure shy wife couldn't possibly have an affair." However, current statistics suggest that 40 to 50% of married women have or will have an affair at least once in their marriage,...although some of these affairs are never fully consummated through intercourse. What's more, and assuming that you've read every page thus far, they arguably have good reason. So, don't be surprised fellas if you've *pushed* your prim, proper and (otherwise) faithful wife to the point where she's become interested and open to other *options*. There is certainly no shortage of available men as similar statistics indicate that 50 to 60% of men are apparently cheating at some point in the marriage and are doing so more than once! In these cases some form of sex (albeit not always intercourse) is usually involved. So, even though we are absolutely positive that each of **our** wives is not capable of such misdeeds,...*she* quite possibly is and most of us are on the other side (with somebody else) as the dastardly enablers!

There's a little more to it for the ladies of course (while not necessarily so for the gents)! Remember, our wives need affection, attention and passion and they long for the days before *ho-hum* became the normal day to day existence. They miss the emotional spark, the loving partner from those early days and someone who will just spend time whispering sweet *nothings* into their ears! Most of all, they want to feel appreciated and needed, not forgotten and frustrated.

These missing admonishments are handily accommodated, although often superficially, through an affair. And, when we think that our spouses are no longer interested in sex,...well, we are right to some degree. BUT, it's usually that they don't want to have sex with us! Women can't get into the mood with someone who brings unnecessary stress into the relationship, lies, is emotionally absent, fails to communicate and generally puts an insufficient amount into the marriage. In fact, these are incredible **TURN-*OFFS*** for married women. So, looking back, as their disenchantment became the norm and they lost interest in sex with their male spouse, but, not with the act itself,...guess what happened? Some other dude *won* them over to an extra-marital tryst. Worse, it didn't take very much effort because the bar was set pretty low by you!

In addition, it is noteworthy that female infidelity is no longer considered taboo. What was once seemingly a male domain, *fooling around* today is now a viable option for many women in an unsatisfying relationship. And, it is not uncommon for the topic to be raised amongst female friends. Wives often seek support, solace and advice from other women when their marriages are foundering. Inevitably, infidelity comes up in the exchange and there is often support for such liaisons. Notwithstanding the existence of peer support or not, if one's husband can't or doesn't provide the support, interest, spark, effort and general companionship that a woman needs, a wife can easily find these things elsewhere. Plus, affairs have a high likelihood of apparent success. They do not generally involve financial stresses, responsibilities or any other such day to day issues.

So, *cheater relationships* definitely appear to have an easier road to apparent (albeit temporary) *success* than do marriages. What's more, not only is the number of cheating wives increasing, but younger women are enjoying the fleeting extra-marital flings as well. It almost seems like once the boredom sets in and the rose colored glasses come off,...anything is possible. Remember gents, many of you have been on the other side! And, although your initial reasoning may have been more physical in nature, you overtly provided all the emotional support that, in fact, your real partner needed!

So, if you think that your wife is cheating, you might find some solace in this. Chances are that any other relationship that your wife might currently be having ultimately has a similar potential for disaster as did yours! Think about it for a moment. Even if the affair has been going on for some time, they really don't know each other very well and there has been little contribution from either party towards a unified existence. No family responsibilities are being undertaken (on behalf of the other or the marriage) as, for example, picking kids up from school, buying groceries, arranging social events, handling household chores, etc. Nor are there any financial stresses on the adulterous affair. For the most part, their clandestine conversations largely surround their respective and *unbearable* home situations and the rest of their *together time* is likely spent in sexual and romantic bliss!

Although in some regards, very appealing, that is far from a solid base for a successful relationship. They haven't experienced any separation/divorce stresses, they haven't gone through the trials and tribulations of getting their kids to successfully interact and they haven't yet experienced any of the day to day relationship stresses that accompany real marriages and real life.

My ex-wife was having an affair with her sports coach (near the end of our marriage). He moved in right after we separated whereupon certain realities set in rather quickly and it became obvious to my ex that he didn't measure up! It wasn't long before she wanted to meet with me to reconcile! So, don't despair,...very often, an affair can be overcome if you are patient and really desire her back.

9) PEER PRESSURE AND MARRIAGE COUNSELING CAN GO EITHER WAY

Peer pressure and other support mechanisms can also affect a woman's decision to leave her marriage. Such peer pressure comes, not infrequently, from insecure, jealous and/or meddling female friends who need to justify their own *less than perfect* lives by bringing those around them down to their level. These *helpful* friends are usually similarly distraught with a multitude of personal and/or marital woes and are often already separated (and unhappily so). This is not to say, by any means, that all females act in this subversive manner when a friend needs support, understanding and a moral compass. But, to be clear, this does occur and NOT infrequently.

In my third marriage/break-up my best friend's wife was so carelessly adamant that I was a bad husband that she not only supported the demise of my marriage, but she made it impossible for my friendship with her husband to continue thereafter. It was terribly unfortunate that her personal insecure predisposition overshadowed my ex-wife's substance abuse as a possible and more likely precursor to the marital problems and ultimate breakdown! Her efforts would have been far more beneficial to all if she had assisted my ex-wife in seeking therapy for her substance problems.

In addition, the world is full of incapable couple's therapists, psychiatrists and marriage counselors who have distressing track records in the area of resolving marital issues and saving marriages. In fact, it is actually easier to find a good car mechanic than it is to find a good relationship therapist! Some counselors have never been married while others are in similarly problematic relationships. Many therapists may not even be entirely unbiased and others simply don't know what they are doing. I have met several who, quite honestly, don't know "an orange from an apple", much less the intricacies of marriage dynamic and I am being kind with those comments! These abysmal practitioners are quite capable of inadvertently steering vulnerable couples down the wrong path. Frequently their own personal lives are so inadequate or in such disarray that they are functionally quite ill equipped to actually provide clear, balanced and effective advice for most real-life marital situations.

Melissa Fletcher Stoeltje, in her New York Times article "The Futility of Couples Therapy", detailed the following comments from counseled recipients,

- "The therapist dispensed what we'd later come to find was boilerplate couples therapy."

- "We'd leave the therapists office rolling our eyes at some comments she'd made."

- "The 20-something therapist, who'd never been married, pinned our relationship troubles on my habit of watching Seinfeld."

Diane Gehart, professor of Marriage and Family Therapy at California State University (at Northridge), states that "many therapists have not been trained to step out of the, *who's to blame dynamic.*"

And, finally, Bill Doherty, Director of the "Couples on the Brink" project at University of Minnesota, has been writing about bad couple's therapy for years. He capsulized five mistakes that inexperienced counselors make (paraphrased by me):

- They inadvertently appear to side with one partner or the other.

- They allow spouses to engage in hot conflict during sessions.

- They offer lengthy lectures on better communication skills but little other direction nor substance.

- They all too frequently advise couples to consider trial separation.

- They fail to give proper and clear guidance on issues and homework for each spouse to complete before the next session.

I am not suggesting that all therapists and marriage counselors are incompetent and all marital therapy futile and/or destructive in nature. Certainly there are many good relationship counselors and marriage therapists out there. However, I am providing some added commentary that they are certainly NOT all created equal, the field is poorly regulated and I urge extreme caution when choosing and engaging a therapist. There is no question that poor counseling can lead to further deterioration in a relationship. Accordingly, it is very important to find the right assistance and solicit references that you can verify or risk a continued spiral to divorce.

10) "THE GRASS IS GREENER" SYNDROME

Women are far more likely to leave their marriages when they possess little or no appreciation for what they **do** have, how much they might lose in the process and the efforts required to simply get back what they are about to give up! It is not a pure monetary consideration that is lacking,.....although that is often a good part of the apparent failure. Sadly, many women automatically assume that they will most definitely be in a better *place* and find a happier life in all respects after leaving a marriage and, as such, fail to take proper *stock* (in advance).

This need to *take stock* and analyze the pros and cons of separating (before taking that final step) might seem obvious to you and I or an outsider. But, it is often totally absent in a woman's considerations and thoughts prior to ending a marriage. They are frequently heard to say; "I actually decided I wanted out a year ago but I waited" (as if there is justification laying solely in the fact that she waited a year). Most likely that decision **was** made one year prior. But, the obvious oversight is the failure to properly review, in advance, the consequences of their proposed actions coupled with an adamant desire NOT to change their minds *no matter what*! It seems like many of these separation decisions are made solely on the merits of the marital failings in conjunction with a perceived notion that they can automatically do better and with little regard for any of the current marital benefits.

Interestingly, much of the *reasoning* that women use to justify leaving marriages can be summed up in one simple, but devastating, phrase. It is known as "The Grass Is Greener" syndrome and it is a VERY real phenomenon among disenchanted and discontented wives. "The Grass Is Greener" syndrome invariably becomes a large impetus in marital break-ups and may arguably be the single biggest cause related thereto.

Generally, we seem to have "created" a society where both men and women are so preoccupied with the apparent success of everyone around themselves, that they often lose complete perspective of their own life situations. People rarely relate their lives to those unfortunate individuals who have far less. Rather, the world has created a society of envious and jealous dreamers who are increasingly unsatisfied with their own lot.

Women, in particular, are often consumed with the *incredible* lives led by the elite, renowned politicians, well known public figures and privileged movie stars. The massive sales of tabloid magazines are a testament to that. As the result, it is not uncommon for women to feel that they could have comparatively successful lives and/or that there are better opportunities in other places. Invariably some women pine to return to their *superior* single lives where opportunities were seemingly abound. Others consider such things as their friend's husband being better than their own.

In other words, many women truly and inherently believe that their lives would automatically be better in someone else's backyard! In addition, as these disenchanted married women become more delusional, they also become more emotional and susceptible to change. And, those very two idiosyncrasies fuel the Grass is Greener Syndrome even more!

CONCLUSION TO PART ONE

Women are currently initiating upwards of 75 % of all divorces! My own experiences (3 out of 3) and those that have been related to me by others suggest that when that moment of apparent *no return* occurs, women seem to react as if it is a simple light switch,...one minute they are *in* the marriage and the next minute they are effectively *out* of the marriage. Or shall I say,...**we're out!** When we get our *walking papers*, there appears to be little apparent regard for any of the positive aspects that might have prevailed in the marriage. With a few short words they seem to all but ignore any of the favorable attributes that the marriage might have had as well as any legitimate or mitigating circumstances that might have been present,....like their own shortcomings!

Is that even possible? Don't women take into account the whole picture? Are there no meritable contributions that men make to a marriage? Do men *solely* cause the apparent point of no return in most marriages?

To a large extent, the answer *turns* on the word *solely*. There is no question that an entire book could be written on the sole topic of whether the female marital needs are reasonable, truly attainable and worth it (from a man's perspective). But, once again, the purpose herein is to win her back and not become preoccupied with the legitimacy of the marital requirements placed upon married men. Suffice to say that we are entirely complicit in regards to most marital failings. So much so, that many men can be complete *blockheads* on a good day!

Most men have a hard time recognizing, deciphering and understanding the chain of events leading up to a separation. We are frequently oblivious to even the most reasonable needs of our married spouses. We miss and/or ignore all the signs of discontent and then fail to recognize the various stages of a marital erosion. In other words, we don't do the appropriate things that marriages require and then we fail to see the glaring signs of the resulting demise! Clearly, it took two or three rounds for me to *get it* straight.

So, let me try and put things into a framework that the average 'thick as a brick' guy can relate to. Please excuse me for capsulizing what is probably the most enjoyable part of a new relationship. When we meet someone to which we feel attracted, everyone pretty much starts in the same place,...and by that I mean both men and women. We are bedazzled by the person that we just met,...almost dumb-struck in fact. Every available thought is preoccupied idolizing our new attraction. Then, m*ini-me* takes over the reins for the men as we size up the beauty and physical attributes that present themselves. Women respond more emotionally than sexually. Their thoughts entertain other variables like; "What a *hunk*, I'd feel so safe with him,...and wouldn't we make great babies together!" Finally, both sexes tend to make mental appraisals and evaluations (often within minutes) based upon absolutely no credible information whatsoever. And conclusions are crafted that are more analogous to our last Christmas wish than to anything real or tangible. Worse, as these frequently unjustified fuzzy feelings gain traction, they form the foundations for the next phase of the relationship as both sexes ignore just about every piece of common sense that we thought we had. But, it's the distinction between emotional attraction and physical attraction (and the reasons behind both delusions) that colors our paths further apart.

As I mentioned, men for the most part tend to make initial relationship decisions based upon slightly more physical attributes and women tend to evaluate potential partners from a more emotional, wholesome and motherly perspective. As a man, truly embracing the inherent difference here is difficult. Most men are *nuts and bolts* characters. We have the capacity to appreciate the nuances of emotion. But, we falsely believe that emotion can be broken down and controlled within our sense of order. Men need to be *smacked around* a bit before we properly comprehend the realities of emotions. So, right out of the starting gate, we're off in the wrong direction regarding the most basic element of the relationship. Worse, even when we do better understand the more emotional disposition of women, we tend to give the distinction and the female perspective little or no credibility,...because we are men,...we're tough guys!

Now, I have already detailed at considerable length, how and why married men tend to fall out of vogue with their spouses. I have delineated the likely explanations and reasoning behind a married woman's unfortunate *demise* from a happy marriage to a relationship on the brink. So, I am going to gloss over that segment in the progression of marital break-ups and *jump* to the final dastardly moment of truth itself and what appears to be the actual end of the union.

Men are inevitably surprised (to say the least) when the finale comes and we are effectively shown the exit door. More specifically, we are shocked by the apparent suddenness. We can't believe that it's happening so quickly and we don't understand why she didn't appreciate all the positive things that were accomplished *together*. We feel that, in spite of all the marital difficulties, one minute everything was relatively fine and the next minute completely unbearable for her.

How could she make such a serious decision with such little apparent regard and often without discussing it? We wonder if she's found another man and sometimes she has. But, that is rarely the underlying reason for the break-up. Very simply, we are shell shocked and reduced to mush in that moment. But, should we be so shocked? Probably not!

The simple reality (gents) is that the decision (to separate) wasn't the result of a *five* minute cursory review by your spouse and hatched in a vacuum. The final decision wasn't made quickly or with total disregard to any positive parts of the marriage. In fact, everything has most likely been far from relatively fine leading up to the bad news.

In contrast, the *sudden* decision (to separate) probably had origins months if not years before. There would have been a massive build-up of problems, frustrations, issues, stresses, emotions and negative feelings which ultimately triggered and fueled your wife's inherent demise into total (marital) unhappiness. Any combination of general boredom, lack of support, loneliness, insufficient communication, mid-life erratic hormones and (the decisive marriage killer) falling out of love would have taken their toll on your wife's psyche (with devastating results) over a considerable period.

In fact, by the time that the final stage of "falling out of love" passes, women have very little distance to travel to the point of *dictating* separation,....the marital fate having been long since sealed! Fear not however, in Part 2 you'll learn all the steps necessary to (with a little bit of luck) win her back!

PART TWO – THE SECRET PLAN FOR WINNING HER BACK

Well, there you have it gents,...the ten basic reasons that might explain your wife's desire to separate. Many of these explanations also shed light on why so many women appear to *blindly* leave marriages that sometimes appear otherwise as *not so dysfunctional* in so many other respects. Moreover, there is good reason as to why I went to such lengths to provide that prolonged back-drop of information. Your understanding, appreciation and efforts to rectify the reasons (for her leaving you) will be integral to the success of winning her back. In fact, with that information in mind, the next part is a simple game plan.

If you purchased this book, and read Part 1, you know that at least 4 or 5 of the ten separation reasons (detailed in Part 1) were probably responsible for or at least contributed to the demise of your particular relationship. And you were complicit in all of them.

So, what is this *secret* plan for winning your partner back? Well, firstly, you'll find that it probably begins in the exact opposite way that you might have imagined. Your first inclination is to tell your wife that you want to talk things through (and fix *it*). You want to beg for forgiveness, offer to change (all your nasty habits and shortcomings), plead with her to stay and engage her in communication to address the problem.

Unfortunately, none of those actions, at this early stage following a separation, will work nor amount to anything positive. Trust me. I tried them all and failed. Plus, many others have tried before you and almost ALL have failed as well. Your wife probably took an undoubtedly lengthy time frame (possibly years) to get to the point where she verbalized her desire to separate. So, she's not likely to reverse that decision in any short order just because you *promise* to change! And, if you pursue any of those courses of action at this early point in time, you will most assuredly make your position worse. In fact, even if she has asked for a divorce,...simply say, "OK" because, in reality, your marriage is not necessarily at the end! But, any 'in her face' attempt to resolve things now will deteriorate your position and reduce your ultimate chances of winning her back at a later date.

This book is *not* about a short term quick fix that suits all and resolves all. It is entirely about those genuine men who are prepared to figure out what happened, set their egos aside, identify their responsibilities and change the negative attributes that contributed to and/or caused the problems in the first place.

This book is about long term improvements and raising oneself to a higher level. In other words, this book is about helping people who really want to help themselves and put in the required effort to accomplish those changes. If you are true to your mission statement (of reconciling with your ex), you won't cut any corners nor look for ways to speed up the process. In the overall scheme of life, it is a relative small commitment of time and effort.

Keep in mind also, that your immediate desire to try and *fix* things, no matter what it might take, is quite honestly a "knee-jerk" reaction to the emotional trauma of separating. All of a sudden she's *gone* or you are packing your bags for a hotel. Your head is spinning with thoughts like "I want her to stay", "What about my kids", "I can't deal with all this and work too", "Where will I live", "I can't afford this", etc.

So, it is quite normal to feel the extreme urge to immediately *fight back* in an effort to return everything to the prior status quo. You want to beg, plead and try and coerce her to *stay*. Unfortunately and at this moment, any hope of things returning to normal in short order is quite unrealistic. So, stop trying to change her mind or her feelings towards you. You will only make things worse and in so doing, the process of reconciling more difficult. Take a deep breath, *suck it up* and get used to your new (and hopefully temporary) state of affairs. Try to remain stoic and fight the urge to do anything other than setting up your new life.

The road to a possible reconciliation is a process and a good part of the process involves recovery, personal enhancement and redevelopment programs. So, you must allow the necessary time for its appropriate implementation.

I cannot stress enough, that you should do absolutely nothing in regards to your marriage, the break-up and your ex-spouse immediately following a separation. Nothing rash, nothing stupid, certainly nothing illegal and most of all,...nothing that you'll regret. Think everything through carefully before you act particularly as you want her back. Rationally, you don't want to undermine the process of winning her back. So, try and resist any urge to react.

I can tell you for sure that, having a restraining order issued against your coming within half a mile (of your ex) will not be considered a positive step in trying to win her back! Spend the short term future on **YOU** and only **YOU** (with the singular exception, of course, being your children).

So, with the high level objective that you want to win your ex-wife back, there are four general steps that need to be taken and we will cover all of them, in detail, in this part of the book. To give you an idea as to where we are *going*, I've summarized these steps below with some brief insight beyond as well.

The Secret Plan For Winning Her Back

1. FIRSTLY, THERE NEEDS TO BE A *COOLING* DOWN PERIOD.

You need to allow time for your ex-spouse to *hate* you less and really appreciate her new *preferred* situation. There needs to be a 4 to 8 month time period (and possibly more) during which there is no face to face contact and if possible no contact whatsoever. At minimum, there should be severely limited and non-personal communications (preferably by text and/or E-mail) and only when absolutely necessary.

Trust me, her new life is going to be a whole lot *less perfect* than that which she probably imagined (prior to the breakup) when she was busy *despising* you. So, don't provide legitimacy to her reasons for hating you! Don't do anything rash or foolish. Remember the old adage,..."Out of sight, out of mind" and that will work very well for you at this early stage. She chose the 'bed' that she's now in,...so, let her have the opportunity to truly appreciate it! At some point during this *cooling* down period, your ex-wife will, most likely start to realize that the *grass is not at all greener* in her new existence. The children might be occupying an inordinate amount of her time, money will likely be in shorter supply and any new relationship (or continued affair) will start to take on much the same normal real life stresses and responsibilities that probably existed in your marriage. But, during this period, you won't be the culpable party because you won't be around interacting and communicating (unnecessarily) with her. Additionally, **you** need time to recover as well. So, be patient and don't rush the process.

2. YOU ARE GOING TO OVERCOME YOUR LOSS AND REGAIN YOUR CONFIDENCE THROUGH ENJOYABLE DIVERSIONS.
Your spirit has likely been badly bruised and you have probably taken a serious psychological and emotional *hit*. It is therefore important that you implement a recovery and *rebuilding* process, during which you divert any negative energy and thoughts to more positive and enjoyable activities like hobbies and dating. You need to regain your self-esteem and these sorts of activities are huge confidence builders. Plus, they can be a lot of fun as well. It might also be appropriate to seek out profession therapy to assist you through this period. Not only is there no shame in seeing a therapist, but it will assist in accelerating your recovery. You are stronger than you might believe and capable of much more,....but you do not need to do this alone! Either way, you need to re-establish yourself and return to 100%!

3. YOU ARE GOING TO CREATE A NEW AND IMPROVED 'YOU',....
a repentant but happier person with an improved disposition, higher values, a positive attitude and an upgraded external image. That's right you are going to embark on a complete makeover that will both surprise and intrigue your ex. In short (and if you follow the advice in this book), you are going to transform yourself into a genuinely better person and one that is considerably more desirable to the opposite sex in general!

4. FINALLY AFTER 4 TO 8 MONTHS, THE NEW 'YOU' WILL INITIATE

***CASUAL* INTERACTIONS WITH YOUR EX-WIFE.**
But, do not proceed to Step 4 unless you have *all your ducks in order*. In other words, make sure that you have properly completed everything to this point. With that in mind, the significant variance in time (4 to 8 months) is more about the time it will take **you** to complete those first three steps properly. However, under no circumstances should you embark on this 4th step before four months have passed as your ex will undoubtedly not be ready. Moreover, if you complete all three steps (by the fourth month) and still see signs of rejection, do not attempt to interact. It is critical that you wait until she is, at minimum, neutral towards you.

Once you have a checkmark beside each of the first 3 steps, you will orchestrate a first *chance* interaction with your ex. It need not be a lengthy first encounter but, it does need to appear unintended. This will be your opportunity to *advertise* the new and improved **you**. Thereafter, you will find other reasons to have two to three additional *chance* encounters. During these physical interactions you are going to subtly present a new opportunity to your ex, namely you. In addition, you will implant the impression (with your ex-spouse) that you might be taken off the market by a new (younger) partner!

Complete each step. Finally, it will be the gents who complete each step thoroughly, move forward slowly and do not rush any part of the process that will more readily reach their desired goal. It will be those individuals that are patient, self-critical and genuinely interested in becoming better people that will be the true benefactors of this program. So, my best advice is to cool your jets and be prepared to put in a genuine effort over the next few months. The rewards will be well worth it as you realize the real and positive changes in yourself. So, let's get started.

STEP 1 - NO UNNECESSARY COMMUNICATION OR ENABLING (FOR A MINIMUM FOUR MONTH PERIOD)

Once the actual separation has begun, you must stop interacting with your ex, stop engaging her and simply stop communicating with her entirely if possible. It is not about being mean and it is not about retribution. There simply needs to be a *cooling* down period for both of you. Your emotions will be *running high* and it is critical that you neither do, nor say anything that might be counterproductive to winning her back. Your break-up may have happened under very bad circumstances. Nasty verbal exchanges may well have taken place. Your ex-wife might even have espoused that she doesn't love you any longer. More than likely those words were not entirely heartfelt and undoubtedly the result of extremely elevated emotions. But, you do not want to make the situation worse by continued dialogue and/or heated communications. She will be much more receptive to communicating with you after emotions (on both sides) have wound down! And by then, you will be otherwise prepared.

Alternatively, during the separation discussion, your ex-wife may have told you that she, in fact, *still has feelings for you* and possibly she does. But, don't misconstrue that overture for an invitation to beg her to stay. Be patient, as there will be a much better time and opportunity later. Nonetheless, she is almost surely not interested in hearing any pleas for mercy at the moment. She has already made up her mind and you will only undermine your ultimate efforts of winning her back should you attempt to do so prematurely. Plus, if you try now, you'll invariably degrade yourself in the process. There is no mileage in your ex-wife's opinion of you being further diminished by your begging. No woman truly desires a wimp! Save the few tidbits of positivity until (much) later after you have rebuilt and regrouped for a comeback.

Remember also that, she likely sees you as *negative energy* and a problematic entity in her life right now and it will take some time to dispel that notion. Constantly injecting yourself inside her daily routine will only accentuate that perception. So, you want to do just the opposite and make yourself scarce immediately. You want to be "out of site and out of mind" as soon as possible. Effectively, you want to "fall off the face of the earth", at least as far as your spouse is concerned, for the next four to eight months minimum. Only then will the *dust* have settled and the possibility of return present itself.

Should she call for something in the early weeks (and she might if you have been an enabler in any way), don't take the call. Return those calls with SHORT, POLITE and NON-EMOTIONAL texts saying, "How can I help you?" Under NO CIRCUMSTANCES should you engage her in unnecessary conversation. And, under no circumstances should *you* initiate any communication except as it might relate to the custody, visitation and/or care of your children. Essentially, this period immediately after separation is a **NO CONTACT** period.

It is important to remain level headed and embrace the *cooling* down period as being vital to the process. It is not about being unreasonably harsh to your ex and I am not suggesting such a course of action. It is about having a plan and being focused on your goal of winning her back. Accordingly, it's important that you not lose sight of your task! Plus, you would find communicating and interacting with her painful at this stage as she'll likely treat you more like a carrier of some contagious disease than a husband! And, she needs time to recover and reflect as well! Her negative feelings towards you will likely abate with time whereupon your chances of reconciling will be vastly improved. Plus, once you implement the NO CONTACT *rule* with your ex, you'll likely appreciate a major reduction in stress and aggravation. You'll enjoy a significantly more positive and therapeutic existence as well. In fact, your entire emotional recovery will be much quicker.

In addition, it is necessary for you to stop *protecting* her, stop helping her and essentially STOP *BEING THERE* for her (should that have been the case during the marriage). Don't enable her new situation as it does not support your goal of winning her back. In fact, it allows her to have her cake and eat it too! I had a good friend that, at the simple bequest of his ex-wife, continued completing her tax returns for years! And, although he always remained hopeful, they never got back together.

Your spouse must lose all the things that she might have taken for granted in your relationship and I'm referring more (but not exclusively) to the non-monetary things. Otherwise, how can she begin to appreciate those things (that she gave up) if you keep providing them? She must lose them all and only then might she reflect on their value. In time she will start to think about more of the positive things that you **did** bring to the marriage and hopefully less about your marital failings and the reasons that prompted the separation!

In the early days, weeks and months after the split, constant communication will only remind her of all the negative things about the relationship. The mere sight of you (and/or hearing your voice) will probably conjure up many negative feelings and, as she is likely NOT yet on 100 % firm ground (with her decision to separate), these overtures will be counterproductive serving only to reinforce her decision to *part company*. Don't give her more reasons to stay separated! Embrace the **NO CONTACT** rule.

Accordingly, do not call, do not text and do not E-mail. Don't send flowers, chocolates or sweet letters of explanation, remorse and/or regret. Equate communication with NEVER getting back together. Don't keep *tabs* on your ex through her friends and/or relatives as you do not want it getting back to her that you are in any way still interested! Keep your distance no matter what; don't follow her (even though you will feel the urge). I did and it was most humiliating! Don't hang around the *corner* from where she is living (post separation),...especially if it is your (old) house. I did that too and it was demeaning and embarrassing!

During this early period of separation, I recommend that you assume the rule that "silence is golden." Barring the need to communicate in regards to the children's interests and assuming that there is neither a fire nor your untimely death,...stop looking for reasons to talk to your ex-spouse. Garner new *head space* that takes you in exactly the opposite direction. Get used to the idea of NOT TALKING to her and not communicating with her. When responsibilities surrounding the kids require interaction, do so briefly, politely **and by text or email only**. And, don't knock on the door when you are picking your children up for your weekend. They know what your car looks like!

A simple but effective exercise is to set a target for the length of time that you believe you can go with NO DIRECT CONTACT whatsoever. At the beginning, set the target at three or four days and try to realize it. Whenever there is a reason to communicate, find a way around it. Use one way texts like, "I'll pick the kids up from school at four today." Don't engage a conversation by asking her what time you should pick the kids up. And, use other people if you need to exchange items. Once you successfully accomplish the first (timeframe) goal, extend it and see if you can accomplish a longer period without direct contact. And, so on,....

Do **NOT** advise your ex-spouse that you are going to adhere to this *no contact* policy. Just do it. Should she call, just respond with a short polite text. "Is there something that you need?" If she requests a favor that does not involve your children, politely decline advising that under the circumstances it would be better if she handled things herself.

Remember, she requested the separation and separations should not include marital type patronages! Advise her that it is painful for you. Should she (by some miracle) want to talk about the marriage, respond by text that you would welcome the opportunity after you've had a chance to recuperate and recover from the ordeal.

But, in that latter circumstance, I strongly recommend (to ensure a positive outcome) that you continue reading this book and complete as many of the suggestions as possible before getting together.

At some point (probably earlier rather than later), certain realities regarding your ex-wife's new life are bound to set in. Moving, especially under these circumstances, will not be a pleasurable process no matter which party is vacating the matrimonial home. And, uprooting children is very distressing as well.

If your ex is the one leaving, she will feel heightened levels of stress and anxiety (especially if she wants to get out of there) immediately after delivering the bad news. Finding a place to live is never easy. It will take time to check listings and view potential accommodations. Plus, extra funds will clearly be required and rarely can a move happen immediately. So, you may still be occupying the same residence during the first weeks and/or months of separation. My first wife and I cohabitated for almost one year after she expressed her desire to separate! We had an infant son,....so separating was not a viable option at that moment. It made the **no contact** rule difficult to implement while we remained living in the same house!

However, once the move has actually occurred, the **no contact** rule should be maintained as much as possible and even in awkward situations. One of you will undoubtedly have left things behind that you forgot or simply that you want to store. Be kind and cooperate but find an alternate person to acquire or *hand off* any of those items so that the **no contact** rule can be maintained. It will be a huge benefit later.

If you are the one moving out, your ex will still find the event painful and somewhat tormenting as will you and your children (who hopefully will not be present). There is always one small part of your ex-wife that will bear (and arguably so) some of the responsibility for breaking up the family. She will feel anguish, sympathy and regret. But, do not attempt to avail yourself of the perceived opportunity and do not console her as she still feels a lot of anger towards you, the one she considers primarily responsible! Do what you need to do in as far as vacating the premises and let it go at this time.

Try very hard to ignore the emotions of the moment, both hers and yours. It will be difficult,...but, it is possible if you find that inner strength to *rise above* the situation. Try to console yourself in the fact that you believe that the breakdown was not entirely your fault. For example, in most cases, there are other options to address marital problems (other than separation) and her failure to properly seek them out places considerable blame on her. It might not be entirely accurate,...but, it will get you through the day. Hold onto whatever positive thoughts or disposition you need to keep a level head!

The bottom line here is that your wife is going to feel a certain sense of unhappiness and loss upon your departure as well (even though she might *hate* you at the moment and has probably verbalized same) and if you really desire reconciliation, you'll want those feelings of remorse to linger. So, don't ruin it by reacting like a juvenile delinquent or madman!

To summarize, you must end all communication immediately (but nicely because you don't want her to think that you're an total ass,...but rather just getting on with your life as she undoubtedly instructed). In fact, write her a short note after you move out and tell her that it *hurts* when you see her and talk to her so you are going to stop communicating directly (unless absolutely essential) and try and move on with your own life. She will be relieved to hear that (for the short term). In reality, you must, in fact, move on with your life in every regard including dating as there is no guarantee that you will re-unite. And, you must wait at least four to eight months before finding a reason to cross paths with your ex-spouse and only after you have undertaken all the suggestions in this part of the book.

Following the physical separation, there will likely be a period during which your ex-wife realizes that several things (that she might have overlooked) were lost in the separation,...assuming, of course, that you weren't a complete dud and did, in fact, put something of consequence into the marriage. Call it a partial awakening point for her. Possibly, you did a lot of the household chores and cut the grass or did the grocery shopping and regularly picked up the kids from school. Or maybe you were the primary income earner, arranged the mortgage, handled her tax returns and/or paid the combined bills. Whatever those things might have been, your ex-wife will now have to handle them herself and on her own.

Do not, under any circumstances, continue to undertake ANY marital function or responsibility (except with regards to children), that was commonplace when you were living together. There is a simple truth to be had here,...she wanted to be on her own,...well, let her experience life's realities on her own! Do NOT help or facilitate in any way as there will be no reward for your efforts downstream! To be clear, I did not say to be nasty or cruel. I simply advised you to let your ex-wife experience her new life as she apparently wishes,...meaning, without you!

It will be difficult for her and stressful for sure,...and for you as well. However, unless the two of you have millions of dollars, her standard of living (and yours) is inevitably going to be adjusted downward almost immediately as well as in future. Whatever you each enjoyed before the separation,...you are going to enjoy less of in future,...theoretically, and once assets are divided,...it will be one half! In the interim, I STRONGLY urge you NOT to enable her more than you are ethically and legally bound (see the next chapter on "Money & Financial Obligations"). Remember that **she** chose the path of separation. So, do not make it financially easier for her than it is supposed to be. As I mentioned, you too will suffer financially and likely more so! Unless you are in the top 10 to 15 percentile of financial earners, you too are going to be forced to change your lifestyle appreciably. Clearly, it is far more expensive to run two households than one!

Accordingly, do NOT give her more money than you have to by law. GET OUTSIDE PROFESSIONAL ADVICE and let an arbitrator or lawyer be the *bad guy* (and bearer of any disconcerting monetary news to your ex). If you were the primary income earner and you really want her back, you can't give her *the cake* (otherwise known as the separation) AND the icing as well (the ease and ability to continue her previous standard of living after the separation). If you do enable her in this area, it will definitely become one massive reason for her NOT to reconcile,….ever!

The underlying insight here is simply that the door might begin to open for your ex-wife to consider a different perspective of the failed marriage once the financial and other realities set in. Recognizing these realities prior to separating would have been difficult when she was consumed with overwhelming feelings of disenchantment, lack of appreciation and anger toward you and the marriage. Moreover, and as time moves on, she might start to question (herself) as to whether her reasons for opting out of the marriage were well founded in the first place. Suffice to say that *cracks in her armor* might well begin to manifest rather early in the separation.

But, don't react just yet. Give the separation and life a chance to play out further. Time may well be a big benefit to you and your goal. Accordingly, I recommend again that you maintain a **NO CONTACT** philosophy, remain *distant* and removed and do not attempt any efforts of reconciliation at this time. You should endeavor to maintain a detached (but respectful) **NON** relationship regarding everything except your children. Your job is no longer that of a considerate husband and you apparently didn't do so well in that regard in the first place (when you were together) or you wouldn't be on the outside looking in now! So, don't try to be attentive at this stage. Be patient, the appropriate time to make your *move* will come.

WHAT ABOUT MONEY, FINANCIAL OBLIGATIONS & SETTLEMENT?

First and foremost, seek the advice of legal counsel immediately. If your ex has already served you with legal *papers*,...you have no choice but to seek counsel. More likely she hasn't and you should solicit advice on your own so that you better understand your financial rights and obligations. Suffice to say that, this is a serious but, contentious and complicated topic that will only be mentioned superficially here. So, please seek professional advice. You need not advertise (to your ex) that you are seeking proper, outside advice. But, do so nonetheless.

In the interim, if your ex-wife was the primary income earner in the relationship, you probably don't need to do anything at this time aside from talking to a lawyer. Similarly, if each of you independently earns a substantial amount of money, you likely don't need to do anything at this time (except, once again, seeking proper legal advice). If however, the family income was average and more evenly derived or you were the substantive *bread winner*, than you have an obligation, morally and legally, to provide financial support for your ex-spouse and your children to ensure their continued economic status quo.

So, my simple advice is to do the right thing **before** it becomes an issue and/or a binding court directed requirement. Having your wages garnisheed is embarrassing for sure and no picnic to deal with thereafter. So, make the right financial arrangements immediately upon separation! If your spouse was an average, equal or lesser income earner (when compared to your income), you must provide sufficient funds so that she (and your children) have similar shelter, food, education and spending money to that which they had before the separation. Different countries, states and provinces will have different legal intricacies. But, all westernized *family support structures* are based upon a similar theme. Your local lawyer or solicitor will be able to direct you more specifically.

Unfortunately, for most men who are the primary or 50 % income provider (of the family), these support payments often provide a hardship that is difficult to deal with,...especially at the outset. Nonetheless, *support* (following separation) is the underlying moral philosophy of western society as well as being engrained in the legal systems,...so, start writing weekly post-dated checks (and make sure that they don't *bounce*). Don't try to *cut corners,* or you will likely (and rather quickly) be on the wrong end of a *screaming* ex-wife, legal letters (from her lawyer) and/or garnishees of your earnings (funds which will be taken directly at the source). Furthermore, if you fail to make her new existence fairly and reasonably transitional, your downstream plans of winning her back will be handicapped to say the least.

Things might have to be sold! You might have to entertain a roommate or additional part time job or some other measure of financial supplement. It likely won't be a pleasant *walk in the park* unless you are in the top 10 to 15 % of income earners. After separating from my first wife, I had to take in a roommate AND find a part time job to supplement my income!

In summary, I cannot urge you enough to start writing those weekly post-dated checks,...one (child support) check for your children and one (spousal support) check for your wife. Inscribe onto each check the exact purpose for same (spousal support or child support) and make both payable to your ex. However, under no circumstances should you provide funds by cash, bank transfers or any other electronic delivery. There must remain a clear and easily identifiable record of all your payments **AND EXACTLY WHAT THEY WERE FOR**. I had an ex-wife who stood up in court and unequivocally advised a judge that I had not given her a dime in over a year. Fortunately, I had over fifty redeemed checks in hand each clearly marked with its purpose and the amount!

In addition, it is important to neither over-provide nor under-provide financially. Once again, professional input can steer you to the right plan. The post-dated checks are best delivered by courier so that you have a receipt of delivery as well. And, that will eliminate and/or minimize unnecessary contact with your ex-wife. Give her a three month supply of postdated checks.

With regards to the (ultimate) splitting of assets (those items like cars, stocks/bonds, real estate, cash, jewelry, household items, etc.), I would suggest, subject to your lawyer's over-riding advice, that you allow your ex-wife to make the first move. That topic initiates a whole other distasteful process and even if you should decide that you are not interested in reconciling, it serves you little benefit (at this time) to initiate legal processes in those regards (unless you have a new female of interest).

However, you should quietly and confidentially get bona fide third party written appraisals of every asset that you own and/or control that does not have clear and identifiable face value at the time of separation. Assets accumulated during the marriage (like real estate investment properties), and which will be divided equally, are generally deemed to mature on the date of separation. In other words, any increase in value after the separation does not usually need to be shared with your ex. So, it will be important to know later what that asset was worth on the date of separation. The matrimonial home often has some special circumstances and might well be handled in a much different way depending on the jurisdiction in which it is situated. So, once again, I urge you to seek professional advice on all these financial and other matters (including custody and visitation rights of children) and at the same time perform any and all of your financial obligations regarding your family.

WHAT ABOUT MY KIDS?

While no rational, caring adult wants to lose *full time* custody of their children, it is more often the unfortunate consequence for men coming out of a marriage and into separation. Current western family law perspectives are frequently far from truly equal and certainly not entirely fair. They frequently dictate results that place a hardship on separated husbands. In addition, women are well aware of the inequity and often use it for self-serving reasons.

So, you might as well get used to the idea as soon as possible. There is no sense in getting your feathers ruffled on this topic as it will accomplish nothing (except aggravating an already difficult situation and upsetting everyone involved). With luck your ex will be reasonable in as far as visitation arrangements with your children. But, be advised that many women do not act reasonably in these regards especially at the start of a separation. Worse, some women use the children and visitation as a means of retribution and to exercise power over you!

Accordingly, you might experience a significant sense of "loss" related to your children as well as having to endure a whole host of other distressing emotions related to the breakup. Nonetheless, you need to make the mental sacrifice quickly so that your wellbeing and your children's wellbeing are not compromised further.

In fact, the effect of marital breakdowns on children is the most difficult to accept. Clearly the children did nothing wrong. Yet, they are the real casualties of marital demise and separations. Children of all ages will feel a multitude of highly negative and confusing emotions upon the separation of their parents. They will experience guilt, extreme sadness, a sense of loss and even abandonment as one parent is no longer in their day to day lives. They will also feel somewhat responsible for the possibility that they might have caused or contributed to the separation. All these feelings significantly raise their level of stress and anxiety beyond any reasonable threshold for children. So, although you are undoubtedly going through a very bad time yourself, it is critical that you try and do what's best for your children,...the *wee* ones and the older (adult) ones alike. The traumatic effects of spouses breaking up can be equally felt at all age levels.

Due to the stresses of the moment and the trauma caused by the separation to all involved, you might think it better to create distance between you and your children. But, under no circumstances should you estrange yourself from your children. Unless ordered otherwise by a court of law, try to spend **more** time with your children then you did before. If they are upset and do not wish to see you, give them some *space*, a short time period to reflect and then try to open a dialogue (again). Keep talking to them until they agree to engage with you. If you are unable to resolve the situation, seek counseling for you, your children (and your wife if she is agreeable) to resolve the visitation issue.

While I do not pretend to be a child psychologist, nor any other authority in that area, I will make some suggestions as to how best to provide for your children during these upsetting, distressing and agonizing times. First and foremost, it is important (if possible) that you and your ex-wife come to a clear understanding and agreement regarding reasonable custody and visitation rights. If possible, those arrangements should be made before you advise the children of your intentions to separate. Unfortunately, many ex-wives and mothers dictate the terms surrounding custody and visitation pretty much eliminating any input from you or your children. While the chances of altering those unilateral resolutions are slim, I do suggest that you seek the advice of counsel to help you resolve issues of this nature.

However, should the topic of custody and visitation be more open to discussion (with your ex) consider the following approach. Unless you have already agreed to share custody AND kids time equally, it might be advantageous (I think that it is) that the children have some *voice* in as far as with which parent they will be spending the majority of their time. More particularly, older children might theoretically be given a larger *speaking* part in this regard (than younger children).

Sadly, and as you can imagine, the topics of custody and visitation are fraught with potential pitfalls, opposing interests and sometimes unachievable objectives especially when the number of individuals involved (in the decisions) increases. And, that is the case when everyone is acting reasonably! So, as many separations are acrimonious, tread lightly and try and communicate sanely and ethically with your spouse. If necessary and both parents are in agreement, seek professional counseling. But, always try to place your children's needs above your own. Remember, like yourself, the children didn't choose to separate,...so, they do not deserve to be put in the middle of your difficult situation or otherwise unduly traumatized. Here are some additional pointers (regarding your children) that can be helpful through the separation and afterwards.

- Do not argue in front of your children.

- Do not diminish your spouse in front of your children.

- Try to maintain a single parental front (with your ex) in the after separation child rearing endeavors.

- Make sure that your children **KNOW** that you both love them. TELL THEM REGULARLY and reassure them. Tell your children that things will work out and demonstrate confidence.

- Don't ever put your children in a position where they need to support you emotionally.

- Tell your children that the separation has nothing to do with them AND is NOT their fault in ANY way. Ensure that your children feel neither responsibility for the marital breakdown nor any responsibility to fix the situation!

- Do not involve your children in disagreements with your ex. Avoid situations where you or your spouse becomes combative in front of the children. Don't put your children in the position where they MUST choose you or anything else that might be integral.

- Try and continue all of the children's current routines and activities. Continue their after-school and other events without interruption.

- Choreograph the conversation (wherein you tell your children about the pending separation) in advance. Ensure that the reasons you give for the decision to separate are both believable and blameless. Have a united front (even if you don't want the separation) with your ex if possible. Be prepared to have to repeat the reasons for the separation multiple times over the coming months and years. Prepare for their questions and have acceptable answers. Be cognizant that older children will require more detail surrounding the separation as well as the logistics that might affect them. Explain that the separation is not the fault of either parent, even if you think that it is! Tell them that you love them and that neither parent is stepping out of their lives,....only that new living arrangements are being put in place.

- Most children will exhibit signs of distress upon hearing the separation news. Acknowledge your children's feelings whether they do or do not demonstrate anxiety at this moment. Allow your children to speak and be heard. Be prepared to try and accommodate some of their verbalized concerns and/or desires. Explain that there may be some minor changes but that most of their routine will be maintained.

- Provide a consistent, unified, amiable and non-stressful environment for your children throughout the separation and afterwards.

- Have multiple conversations with your children before the separation and afterwards. They will have new concerns and questions as things evolve.

- Don't underestimate the severity of the impact on your children and be prepared to do whatever is necessary to minimize the negative effects.

- Try to emulate the perfect parent that you might like to have if you were a child in similar circumstances. Don't display any of your negative emotions or feelings surrounding the breakup. Display a sense of strength, security, confidence and normality.

- Make sure that you remain **there** for your children no matter what! Make sure that you tell them **and** that they understand that neither parent is abandoning them.

- Ultimately your children will want you (both) to succeed, to be happy and to 'flourish' in your (new) life. In the interim however, there will be much anxiety. Don't give them cause to doubt or lose hope in you. In other words, don't be a failure. Cope (as necessary behind your mask of misery) and provide the sense of strength and security that your children need to see. If you are distraught over the separation, remain stoic in front of and for your children. You can show disappointment and remorse (regarding your loss) and are permitted to be human but not weak.

- Introduce new, happy routines and activities in which you and your children participate.

- Deal with **your** sense of loss, insecurities, guilt, anger and other emotions privately and when your children are not around.

- Do not exhibit malice or other negative emotions when referencing to your ex-spouse. Always demonstrate a positive outlook in front of your children.

- Ensure that your wellbeing is continually addressed as well. The results will be obvious and have a positive effect on your children.

- Your children have the right to be angry too. Give them that right and the opportunity as well. Do not be unreasonably responsive and/or harsh should these emotions be demonstrated by your children.

- Be cognizant of consequential changes in your children's behavior and seek the advice of a professional should any appear to be substantive and/or as you deem appropriate.

It is important during this period that you maintain a healthy relationship with your children. In fact, it is an opportunity to strengthen that relationship. Try and see them as much as possible and whenever agreeable to your ex. However, it is equally important (if you truly hope to reconcile with your ex) that you maintain distance from your ex-wife, sever physical interactions with her and communicate only by text or E-mail as might be necessary (for your kids).

You can get through this in one piece for sure. So, can your kids. Moreover, if you minimize the *damage* and mental anguish caused to your children, it will be a *win win* result for everyone. Your children will weather the storm better and it will most definitely assist you in the pursuit of winning your spouse back.

STEP 1 - SUMMARY AND REVIEW

Before I proceed and because of the incredible importance of Step 1, I think that it might be appropriate to summarize the NO CONTACT requirement. Remember, your goal is to win your wife back. So, don't *trip* right out of the gate! It is critical that you embrace and follow the NO CONTACT rule. Accordingly, please don't make the following mistakes. Any one of them could easily set you back considerably, reinforce your ex-spouse's reasons for separating in the first place and spell disaster for your plans of reconciliation.

1) You will feel a significant urge to *talk* your way out of the separation especially in the first minutes, hours and days after you are given *notice* (of the separation). **Don't try**! Don't attempt any *damage control* at this early time. Maintain a **NO CONTACT** policy (right from the beginning if possible) even if physical separation has not yet taken place. Don't buy your ex any gifts under the misguided notion that you might resolve and reverse the situation through apparent coercion. You won't succeed (at this time).

    If you are still under the same roof, don't initiate any unnecessary conversation or interaction. *Move* in the other direction and lead your own life. Give your ex the proverbial 'cold shoulder.' I have a friend that recently separated just before Christmas. As a child was involved and new accommodation not yet acquired, they didn't physically separate for several months. Valentine's Day came along and my friend bought his ex-wife $ 5,000 worth of jewelry in the hope that she would reconsider. She didn't!

    So, keep your dignity, your *head* and your *cool* and don't do anything foolish, illegal or that you will regret. Definitely a tall order! Nonetheless, don't call and text **only** when arrangements for children are in order. Don't go up to her doorstep (even if it's *your* house as well) to pick up your kids on a *Dad's* weekend. Don't talk to her friends or relatives. However, never be rude. So, if contact with her friends or relatives does occur, never inquire, mention or discuss your ex. Create the reality of a communication and physical **barrier** between you. Go deep and GO SILENT my man.

2) Following the initial conversation regarding your wife's desire to separate, don't proposition, coerce or plead for her to reconsider. Should she ask for a divorce, advise her that a divorce is not something you want,...but acknowledge her decision. She won't reverse her decision ***at this time***. But, she can't get a quick divorce so it really doesn't matter. So, don't object and give her time to cool down. Avoid getting into any arguments and/or calling her names (although you will definitely be tempted) because, if you persist, there is a risk that you'll say things even more damaging than you would like. A lot of women will take this opportunity to seek revenge for your causing the marriage to fail (in their view). They will push every sensitive *button* that they can in hopes of causing a reaction and even hurting you. Try and resist. Don't engage her and walk away if necessary when she attempts to upset you. This is a "Yes Dear" moment,...followed by, "If that's what you really want, I guess that I have no choice."

3) Don't lose your shit when you find out that she's dating. The more that you appear not to care, the more she might want you back at a later date (and particularly if ***you*** are dating). It is vital that you take the high road, remain stoic and, at all cost, refrain from expressing your true feelings. It will be intensely difficult and painful for sure. But, the benefits (at a later date) will be equally large one way or the other!

STEP 2 - OVERCOME YOUR LOSS AND
SPEND TIME MOVING IN NEW DIRECTIONS

Get your 'new' life in order based upon the obvious reality that you are now single. In other words, forget the past (for now) and start moving forward to a happy and satisfying existence.

This next step on your 'to do' list is somewhat multi-faceted and serves several important purposes. First and foremost, you need to address the emotional impact of the separation itself. Very likely, your ego was severely damaged, your self-esteem destroyed and your confidence shattered. So, you need to immediately embark on a path that can reverse those things and return your emotional state to a healthy level. The first step is to find things to occupy your time and create distractions so that you are not consumed 24/7 with the loss of your wife and family. You need to regain 100% of your emotional wherewithal. Nothing beneficial will be accomplished if your mental and/or physical health remains broken or diminished.

Begin spending considerably more time with your family, friends and anyone else that will garner *support.* Time spent in those relationships will provide solace, entertainment and deviation from your current norm (of being alone). Other diversions can assist with your recovery as well. Work, hobbies and social activities are great ways to divert and mask negative thoughts.

Very simply, you need to immerse yourself in positive environments so that you have less time to dwell on the past and your separation. Such activities can also reduce anxiety and apprehension created by despair. And, they are excellent mechanisms to raise your confidence level as well. What better remedy or *medicine* (could there be) than going to a baseball game or concert with friends. Your new objective is simply to undertake enjoyable activities that fill the vacancy in your life as much as possible. If you have a hobby, now is your opportunity to spend more time pursuing it. If you like going to movies, see one every week as nothing can be more engaging!

But, don't lock yourself away from people in a misguided effort to be faithful to your ex-spouse or as some form of ill-conceived punishment for your perceived mistakes. Keep in mind that it took two people to get married and two people to create relationship problems. Your wife might have been the one who pulled the *plug*,...but, she was also, more than likely, very complicit in creating the environment that resulted in the separation. So, while you might not feel like getting back *out there*,....it is extremely important that you engage in as much social activity as realistically possible. Accordingly, spend recreational time in areas that involve other people on a regular basis. Wine tasting clubs, basketball, art classes, dance lessons, baseball, cooking classes, language courses are all but guaranteed to make you less cognizant of the past and more focused on the present and future.

This is especially helpful in the case of your ex leaving you for another man, because your "wound" most certainly feels deeper. Rest assured that there is a larger plan and this other guy is, probably less of an immediate threat (than you might think) and more than likely, temporary!

Interact (socially) with colleagues and business friends outside of work. Try and make new friends, particularly ones that you believe your ex-spouse might like and approve of. Attend family gatherings as much as possible. Those close to you will help support you in your time of need. Attend a church or other religious facility and make new friends there. Spiritual activities can bolster fragile egos and mitigate insecurities as well. Seeking spiritual solace doesn't mean that you're going to become a religious zealot.

This step also involves dating even if you don't think that you're ready or it seems somewhat *forced* (at the beginning). Things WILL turn around for you quickly, if you make the effort and give the process a chance! The purpose of dating is three-fold. First, it is a great diversion to your loss and a fantastic confidence builder. Plus, at some point in the future, your ex-wife might well find you more appealing if she *knows* that you are dating. Finally, there is no guarantee that the two of you are getting back together. So, best you start now to (potentially) get on with your life. However, be discreet. There's no need to let your ex (or kids) know that you are dating just yet.

So, dust off your *dancing shoes* and get out there! It is important that you date a minimum of two different ladies and go out on at least eight occasions. Don't be shy or intimidated. You are certainly not without (any) redeeming qualities or your ex-spouse would not have fallen for you in the first place. There will be lots of women who WILL be interested IF YOU MAKE THE EFFORT to put yourself *out there*. In addition, if you use dating sites, the process alone is a great diversion for your sadness and will ease the pain for sure. But, the bonus here is that you will undoubtedly find some very nice ladies with whom you'll potentially want to spend even more time. Worst case scenario,...you might have to choose between reconciling with your ex and a new woman (that might align more to your character and needs). Nothing wrong with that! Consider it as a belated but well deserved, *present* bestowed upon you to offset the rejection by your ex.

I'm not trying to make you feel good here gentlemen by throwing a lot of BS in your direction. If you follow all the advice in this book, you are going to find it relatively easy to attract new ladies and possibly, a number who are somewhat younger than your ex-spouse. They will see you as experienced, stable and mature, often a nice change from many of those lost lads within their age group. All you have to do is put in the effort. When I found myself single (yet again) prior to my meeting my current wife, I barely knew how to turn on a computer. Well, *if the truth be told*, I learned how to use a computer on a dating site and ultimately married the *bonus* in the process!

I can pretty much guarantee that your ex-wife will have a much harder time in this area especially if she is over 40 and/or has custody of your kids. Finding someone to have sex with her will be relatively easy. But, finding someone more permanent will be much more difficult and as the result she might begin to appreciate *her* loss as well!

I have some final words (of consideration and caution) in as far as dating. First, don't be afraid to consider younger women as potential dates. Not too young as you don't want to appear foolish or get the wrong reputation. Certainly keep it legal and realistic in comparison to your own age. But, a good rule is to aim a tad younger than your ex-spouse for sure and eight to ten years younger than yourself. Younger ladies can be more fun and have less baggage. Plus, a younger woman will spark more interest from your ex-wife when the time comes to re-engage communication! My current wife is 9 years younger than myself and 5 years younger than my ex. Interestingly, the age difference is barely enough to accommodate my high energy level.

Nonetheless, under no circumstances should you let your ex-wife (or children) become aware that you are dating *at this time*. It is way too soon. You'll want to be well along in Step 3 before you even consider letting the "cat out of the bag." Plus, it isn't particularly appropriate for you to introduce every new date to your children. In fact, it may never be appropriate (unless a new lady starts to look like a permanent 'fixture' in your life). It is not about lying,...rather, it is about avoidance until a more appropriate time. Don't talk about it and don't flaunt it. Certainly, don't take a date to all the same restaurants, movie houses and other places that you frequented with your ex-wife! If you were caught cheating (during your marriage), this really won't go over well at all should you bump into your ex (or one of her friends). And, if cheating was **not** the reason for your separation, there is still a much more appropriate time to let the dating information *slip*. Be patient.

This part of the program is a real confidence builder and a whole lot of fun. It is an excellent way to get out of any debilitating or depressive moods that you might be experiencing. It is simple and proven therapy (for you). However, if you are feeling excessive bouts of depression, seek help from a qualified doctor immediately. It is important to get back to normal emotionally as soon as reasonably possible. When the time is right for you to attempt to reconnect with your ex, you want to do so from a position of (mental) strength and confidence! So, get out there and enjoy yourself. When I was in this position, I went out with different women twice a week. It was tiring but fun. And, yes there were rejections but I didn't care. I still found myself *in bed* with more than one out of three dates and I'm not a Justin Beiber look-a-like! Here are some brief pointers on regaining your composure and confidence.

HEAL AND MAKE YOURSELF WHOLE AGAIN

- **Stop thinking about what happened**. Stop reliving your failures during the marriage and the ultimate separation. Don't live in the past and don't regret every action you took and decision that you made (prior to the separation). You can't change history. But, you can direct your future! Concentrate on making social plans with friends and family. Organize several outings each week. Arrange and participate in whatever it might be that puts a smile on your face. Engage in anything that provides distraction from the separation and the associated negative feelings.

- If you have a hobby, spend more time pursuing it. If not, spend time considering what new hobby you want to pursue and make arrangements immediately to start. Set aside at least one night each week to engage your hobby.

- Each time you find yourself wallowing in self-pity, force yourself to think of alternative and more positive topics,......things like your new hobby or an upcoming date. Try to concentrate only on positive and uplifting thoughts. Each time you find yourself vacillating towards anything negative,....purposely change the *topic* in mind to something that makes you smile. My *go to* topics are airplanes and waterskiing!

- Seek counseling if you think that it is necessary or beneficial. There is no shame here and it can be incredibly satisfying and helpful. Usually, talking to friends can be soothing as well.

- Join a least one dating site (and possibly two or more) and spend at least one hour per day scanning potential dates, interacting and texting. Within 30 days of your separation, go out on your first date. Forget the notion that you might not feel ready. It's all about the benefits of the *process*. You will likely feel out of place and it may not be the most enjoyable experience at first. You might even feel that you are betraying your wife. You are NOT! This was her ultimate decision,...so, persevere. Go out on more dates as soon as you can arrange them. Within the next four months, you need to embark on no fewer than eight dates with a minimum of two different ladies. Having said that aim for more and elevate your *game* along the way. You need to become secure and confident (again). You can't act like an emotional *basket case*, loser or cad and expect to win your wife back!

- Try to avoid binge drinking and/or binge eating as a source of appeasement to your problems. They will only make things worse, much worse. Embrace a healthy diet. Work out at a gym. It's another opportunity to engage with people.

- Reframe from going to places that you enjoyed as a couple (as much as realistically possible). There are lots of other places around. Checking out new restaurants, theatres, movie houses, bars, etc., is a fun distraction as well.

- In addition to everything mentioned above, try *talking* to yourself about getting strong again. Tell yourself that you can and will get your life back in order. Convince yourself that your confidence will bounce back and life will be happy once again. At this time, you do not need a perfect script for the rest of your life. Simply, act positive and your apparent weaknesses will slowly be replaced by strengths.

- Fight emotional reactions related to the past and your separation. View your previous marriage experience as a learning process. Your state of mind will have a huge impact on the speed of your recovery AND the happiness that does or does not lie ahead for you! Your children need to see strength of character as well. So, don't let them down.

- Go out more frequently with friends and work buddies. There are all sorts of enjoyable and diversionary activities out there. Consider knife throwing (but not at your ex), indoor skydiving, archery tag, flying a simulator, axe throwing (again,...not at your ex), bubble soccer, platform or paddle tennis, rock climbing or a rage room. If you chose one of the above each week, you'll be busy for months!

DATING TIPS

Ok guys, don't get all bent out of shape that I've been leading you down a garden path. We are still heading towards 'winning your ex-wife back',.....assuming that's still what you want! And, you are already half-way to having the necessary tools to accomplish your goal.

But, there are a few more steps and this is one of them,...and it is a critical one. Firstly, you will be far more desirable to your ex (when you make that first pivotal *move*), if she believes that *you* are moving on. Plus, there is a fair chance that you will not reunite with your ex-wife and if that is the ultimate end result, there is no point waiting to get on with your life.

So, be patient....and use the opportunity to work on your image. Get comfortable dating again and enjoy it! As I mentioned, you will be much more appealing to your ex when she finds out that you're dating,...especially if the girl on your arm is younger than she is! Here (in no particular order) are some of the best ways to approach, engage and interest women. And, they will more than likely *work* on your ex (at the appropriate time) as well!

- As mentioned above, **join at least one dating site and preferably two.** Spend at minimum one hour per day on the sites.

- **Be open and honest**. Women who are looking for a relationship, rate honesty and trust (in their partners) as the number one requirement on their *hit* list. But, avoid the topic of your ex-wife if possible especially on the first few date. Should the topic be raised,....nicely and simply respond,......"that part of my life is over and I'm looking for a new beginning." It is very encouraging to most recipients and actually says little. All your options remain open. So, immediately thereafter change the subject. Certainly don't lie. But, get off the topic before you spill your guts and start weeping as she probably won't find that endearing! Do try and project more positive and appealing characteristics. Maybe it's your smile,...maybe it's your ability to listen. Maybe you can tell funny jokes. Figure it out and *use* it to your advantage.

- Ultimately (and after several dates with the same person), should the topic of your ex-wife come up again (and IT WILL),...**your marriage and previous relationship MUST sound over**, even if it isn't (unless, of course, you are *not* interested in any further dates and/or sex with this lady)! Play both ends against the middle with comments like, "I understand that my ex-spouse is having divorce papers drawn up" or "My ex is involved with another man whom she plans to marry." In other words, leave your options open.

- Cleanliness and being well groomed are paramount all the time but, particularly on a first date. And, make sure that you are well dressed. A *classy* look is timeless and unforgettable. **Create a good first impression.**

- **Be polite**, use manners, don't swear and be gracious. These qualities are not passé, nor realms of your parent's era. Thank her for going out with you! No woman will ever criticize a man for being too complimentary and respectful.

- Take the lead on your first date. **Most women prefer guys who take initiative**. That doesn't mean that you should be bossy and/or aggressive. But, few women want a wimpy date or partner!

- **Let your date do as much of the talking as she desires**. Generally that will be a lot! At opportune moments (like when she's eating or drinking) *chime in* with something ***interesting*** about yourself. If you have an intriguing job or pastime, mention that. But, NO BRAGGING under any circumstances. Nobody like a braggart! Women are intrigued by interesting things,...but, not if it involves a lot of bragging on your part. Find a way to slip small anecdotes of interest into the conversation.

- When you do get a moment to tell your date more about yourself, **mention your hobbies and social interests**. Over 30 % of women want to hear about your recreational endeavors and other activities on the first date. But, don't tell your date your whole life story in the first 20 minutes. **Leave something for the second and third dates**. Create some intrigue and mystery by touching briefly on an interesting topic (regarding you and/or your background) and then switching back to letting her talk or to another subject.

- **Avoid talking about sex, religion, politics, future marriage plans and your ex on the first and even the second date** if possible. Such topics are awkwardly sensitive at best and problematic and likely contentious at worst. So, it's best to shuffle them downstream to a point when you might know this person better. You don't want to *walk* onto a topic minefield that you can avoid. Keep the first date (topics) light and positive so that the occasion is relaxing and enjoyable for both parties. If you like her there will be lots of time to discuss touchy and topics on future get-togethers. Plus, you should always ensure that a first date is a pleasurable experience for your companion. Bantering back and forth on a polarizing subject would not be considered a pleasurable first date in most instances! It is the perfect opportunity for you to practice being a nicer person. If, however, your date raises one of these *touchy* subjects, try and keep your response brief, balanced and **neutral**. Don't be the politician who is receptive to everyone's views,....as long as they're similar to yours!

- **Don't text while on a date**. And, don't take selfies unless she asks. In fact, turn off your cell and put it away. It won't *kill* you!

- Most women will *test* you on the first date and ask about your plans for the future, in particular your marriage plans and your interest (or lack thereof) in having (more) children. They want to know (early on) whether your plans coincide with theirs. Be ready with a standard and neutral response like, **"I'm pretty much open to considering anything with the right person."** These questions are not accidental (as your date may well be on a mission to find a mate) and you'd be well advised to remain neutral regarding all of them. And, you won't be lying. Trust me when I say that you have no idea how your life might turn out at this stage. Many men in the exact position as you start out vehemently claiming that they want their ex-wife back and nothing else interests them. But, a year later they are engaged to a great new lady and awaiting divorce finalization.

- If you have some natural talent try to **be humorous** and bring that into the conversation. But, if you can barely tell a tasteless one liner, don't go anywhere near that style. And, it's always best to avoid (humor via) sarcasm in the early stages.

- If you are initially communicating online, **tell her what you like about her profile** and ask her questions along those lines. Then mention some of your interests and hobbies. Try and conclude your communication with something warm, fuzzy and emotionally uplifting such as, "Do you like puppies?'

- **Always be cordial, polite and charming**. Women still love *old school* traditional manners like opening doors, helping them into their seats and picking up the dinner tab. Good manners are NEVER out of date or style!

- **Don't be rude to any third party** on the first few dates,...and that includes the waiter who may have brought you the wrong or cold dinner or the driver who cut you off on route.

- **Don't try and move too fast. You don't need to get laid on the

first date. Well, on second thought,....you might, but, try and slow down anyway (until the second or third date) unless she is steering the ship to a bedroom (in which case, please make sure that you use condoms). I always maintained a 3 date rule for playing the sex 'card' and that worked exceptionally well for me. You won't be a cad on the first date and it keeps them wondering if you are genuinely interested on the second date (giving **you** the *upper hand*)! Of course, I can't deny that my current wife screwed my brains out on the first date. But, it was definitely her idea!

- **Be down to earth**,....even if you are a *tricky dick* high priced lawyer or Wall St financial dude. Don't flaunt any wealth that you might have. Be subtle in that regard and try (first) to determine what kind of person she is,....or you may well be visiting your local dry *cleaners* as there are lots of *gold-diggers* out there!

- **On the first date, offer to meet in a public place** (especially if you *met* online) but let her set the final decision. You want her to know that you are aware of her need to feel secure. Never suggest your place on a first or second date. That is disrespectful and presumptuous. Plus, you don't know *who* you are giving your address to and she probably won't appreciate it anyway. I once stopped dating a girl after the second or third date. At the time, I was living at a friend's place while between marriages. She called one day and (as I was out) my buddy answered the phone. She introduced herself and asked if she might come over to wait for me. He gave her the address and she stalked us both for the next six months!

- **Try to take a first date someplace where you are familiar and comfortable**,...but NEVER any place that you took your ex-wife. She's likely to ask if you've been there before and you *don't* want to answer "yes, with my ex!"

- Find something nice to say at the very outset of your get together. And, I **don't** mean,..."It's a nice day, isn't it." Avoid comments regarding the weather all together. How boring. Flatter her in some way, as for example, "**You have gorgeous eyes**" or "**I like your shoes!**"

- **Bring her a specialty chocolate (in a tiny box) or a single flower**. These items only cost two or three dollars. So, don't be cheap. Give it to her at the beginning of your date so that it sets a pleasant tone thereafter. Keep in mind that women can be just as nervous as we can!

- **Try to do something interesting and different when dating**. Dinner and drinks are almost passé. Try billiards, axe throwing, *who done it* dinner theatre, escape rooms or bowling. Let your fingers do the walking on the internet for ideas.

- Make sure that you are absolutely at the top of your game in terms of *how you look*. **Wear fashionable clothes, nice shoes and be showered and well groomed.** You want to be squeaky clean and upscale trendy. Ensure that you have a small mouth wash in your pocket and use it (in the men's room of course) as necessary.

- If there is a lull in the conversation or you get nervous **have some fallback questions** that you can ask. For example, "What is your most favorite travel destination" or "What hobby would you like to start." It is a good idea to write out some conversation topics in advance and memorize them.

- **Show some chivalry and class. Offer to pay for her UBER ride home**. Certainly make sure that she gets home safely.

- **Confidence comes from repetition.** So, if you *fall off the first horse* (in other words, your date doesn't go so well),...forget it, get back on (by setting up another date with someone else) as soon as possible.

- **Treat your date well.** It's the right thing to do. Treat your date like you would like to be treated even if you don't think that she would make for a good second date! You never know how things might turn out. When I met my current wife, I spent the first hour saying to myself, "there is no way this woman and I are going to see a second date. We are not on the same page." Well, we are now happily married and the marriage has lasted longer than any of the previous three!

- **For every two women that say "no" to a second date,...there is one that will say "yes!"** So, don't be discouraged if someone isn't interested in a second date. If you are following all the dating tips outlined here, you'll be fine.

It is always a good idea to call after a first date especially if you would like to see her again. The reason though, is NOT to ask her out again. You're calling to show that you are polite, caring and gracious. And if you are lacking in those qualities, the call will be good practice.

Remember, you are sincerely trying to be a better person, so demonstrating manners, respect and gratitude is great practice (especially if you have no intentions of dating her again). So, just thank her for a wonderful evening. I generally make this call one or two days after the date. Then, if I like her and if I think she likes me, I call back three or four days later and ask her out on a second date. You never want to appear overly interested, anxious or desperate. Women tend to like a little mystery as long as you're not breaking their hearts! On the second date, bring another small gift (and **nothing** sexual in nature).

Don't get upset or dejected by those women who decline a first date offer. There will be plenty of them that do! Take the position that it's their loss,...because it usually is! Move on immediately to another potential candidate. It's a numbers game. Ask enough women to go out on a first date and there will always be those who say "yes." Don't get unnerved or upset if ten or twenty or even one hundred say "no." Ask one hundred and one!

It goes without saying that dating can be a very pleasurable experience. But, it is also a fantastic confidence booster. And, a high level of confidence will put you in a much better position to ultimately decide whether you really do want your ex-wife back,...or not! As I mentioned earlier, I passed on two occasions with my ex-wives when I had the opportunity. You may well find that there's a new lady in *your* life that interests you more.

In conclusion (to dating), remember the following. When you ask a woman out on a first or second date and she declines, don't get discouraged. There are lots of available women out there. Just keep on trying as it won't take long for you to get into the grove! Once I had dated several women, I maintained a *stable* of two or three different potentials at the same time. That way, if one woman declined an offer to date,...I still had options that were a text away! And, the internet is not the only means of meeting people. Don't be afraid to approach ladies that you meet in every day encounters; like your local bank teller, your waitress at a restaurant, your fitness instructor, your Starbucks server or the admin assistant at your accountant's office. The possibilities are endless. I once asked my son's doctor if she was interested in going out and she said yes.

STEP 3 – TIME TO TAKE PROPER 'STOCK' AND IDENTIFY ALL YOUR FAILINGS. IT'S TIME TO REMAKE YOURSELF!

This is a critical point, a moment of truth when you (**do** look back and) admit to yourself that you were and are far from perfect. Like most people, you have flaws, shortcomings and are guilty of many failings. And, if you are to truly *grow*, you must identify those less than positive traits and mark them for improvement.

Few people have the real capacity to be self-aware. In other words, few people can be truly critical of themselves on an ongoing basis. As part of this process you must become self-critical.

So, you will ignore the shortcomings of your ex-spouse and forget all the frustrating things that she might have done. That exercise will be undertaken later when you ready to make a final decision as to whether you really want her back.

Right now, the emphasis is on **fixing you** and it is vital that you remain focused and honest to accomplish that task. You will need to look in the mirror in a way that you have likely never looked before. You will need to analyze yourself, admit to several shortcomings and then adopt a plan for improvement! Remember, it is not merely about wanting your ex-wife back. It's about improving yourself so that you are a better human being and one that is more appealing to a greater number of people!

So, it is of the utmost importance that you create a genuine list of all your failings as well as the inappropriate behavior and negative conduct that adversely affected your marriage. Of particular note should be the frustrating and annoying things that your wife verbalized (about you). It is important to identify all the habits, character flaws and weaknesses that caused your ex-wife such displeasure that she opted to separate! Chances are that most of your previously unacknowledged shortcomings actually do exist. So, a truthful and impartial list is in order. Add to the list anything that

YOU know (deep down in your heart) should be addressed, changed or stopped. In other words, try to delineate anything that you did (or didn't do and should have) during your marriage that was problematic, created tension, initiated arguments or otherwise upset your ex-wife.

Remember, whether you ultimately win your wife back or move on with another woman (in a new marriage), it is in your best interests to do something about those imperfections, deficiencies and character flaws. Try to be honest and consider all the things about yourself that (probably) don't impress people around you as well. Let me give you a brief head-start with just a few negative traits that average husbands in failed marriages commonly exhibit and which you may have demonstrated during your marriage. Read each one and seriously consider whether it might apply to *you*.

- Were you a lazy and/or complacent spouse who failed to put in the proper effort? If you played a lot of video games, watched sports religiously and/or had trouble holding down a job,...you fit the 'useless' description rather well!

- Were you thoughtless and less than caring? In other words, did you lack empathy and warmth when your ex had an issue?

- Did you avoid daily conversations with your ex-wife? Did you take the time to listen when she wanted to *talk*? How often did you engage her about her day?

- Were you someone who got into a lot of conflicts and/or issues at work or elsewhere during your normal every day routine? Were you a constant source of stress to your ex?

- Were you immature and/or irresponsible during the marriage? Did you act more like a juvenile than an adult? Did you have difficulty taking responsibility for your life? Were you a poor *provider*?

- Were you an ungrateful husband who rarely acknowledged any of your wife's contributions?

- Were you selfish and/or dismissive of your wife's feelings, desires and/or needs?

- Did you drink or take drugs excessively?

- Did you spend a lot of time in front of the television or playing computer games? Were you a sports "nut" somewhat preoccupied by such activities (either watching or participating)?

- Were you unnecessarily unkind, curt, or demeaning or unreasonably sarcastic to your ex?

- Were you unsupportive of your ex regarding her job, goals, hobbies, etc?

- Were you insecure, frequently jealous and/or frequently suspicious?

- Were you overly critical? Were you impatient?

- Did you dress like a slob or a juvenile? Did you frequently look ungroomed? Are your fingernails clean now?

- Were you continually late and/or absent for family functions, meetings, dinners, etc.?

- Did you appropriately contribute to the sharing of child raising responsibilities?

- Did you appropriately contribute to the sharing household responsibilities?

- Were you confrontational, negative and/or overbearing? Were you argumentative?

- Were you unable to provide the emotional support that your ex-wife required?

- Did you have difficulty making the proper commitment?

- Were you irresponsible with money and/or the household finances?

- Did you satisfy your wife's sexual needs?

- Were you frequently away from home or away for extended periods?

Whatever your failings, imperfections and/or weaknesses, it is paramount that you identify them and accept the consequences of *owning* them. Otherwise, it will be impossible to stop and/or mitigate those negative characteristics. So, it is vital that you be as self-critical as possible (at this time) or the next Step 4 will likely fail.

In order to proceed effectively, you will need to be truly remorseful about your failings and character flaws. Remember not only did your flaws contribute to dissolving your marriage but you seriously hurt someone (and someone you loved) in the process. At some point you will need to properly apologize for (all) the mistakes you made as well as the resulting pain that you ultimately caused your wife. But, for now, you need to feel the guilt, accountability and embarrassment. If you are to seriously become a better person, it is paramount that you genuinely regret your behavior and take full responsibility for the consequences of your behavior. In other words, **YOU** must be the one exclusively accountable for the separation! Only then will you be able to properly address your blemishes and only then will you be able to begin building a better character.

Once you have completed your list, you must embark on a campaign that is extremely pro-active and initiate resolutions to your biggest deficiencies. Simply admitting to your shortcomings will not make you a better person. You need to acknowledge the apparent character flaws and create exercises to effectively and genuinely reduce (or terminate) them.

For example, if you are overbearing, you need to spend more time listening to people around you and less time being a know-it-all and/or bossing them around. If you are the jealous type, you need to *suck up* the fact that your ex is probably dating. Consider sending her a card (by mail) wishing her luck in her new relationship! If you are continually late for meetings and functions, you need to learn how to be more considerate of others, less egotistical and more respectful. I don't care who you are or what job you have, being late is completely unnecessary.

Try to create guidelines and rules of ethics for yourself so that you can practice them consistently in everyday life. A simple list of things to do and not do will serve you well. Once created, you should read the list every day,...first in the morning so that you recall the behavioral things that need to be improved. Then, again at night to review exactly how you did. Practice (more frequently) the ones that don't come so easily. Only regular and sustained efforts will bring the desired results. The changes must become habitual. The process requires ongoing concentration, mental input and resolve if you are to effect real improvements.

I think that you should be able to take it from here. I caution you however,...if your list is less than five (**significant**) items long, you are lying to yourself and wasting your time. The only redeeming fact is that you paid me for this book! So, take this seriously. Write down your failings and shortcomings and create daily exercises for resolving them. You can't go forward effectively with exactly the same shortcomings as you had before. Not only will you fail again with your ex-wife (even if given a second chance) but, you'll likely fail in your second marriage (with someone new) as well. If your character flaws include high levels of jealousy, an overly controlling personality, lack of compassion/empathy or low levels of confidence/self-esteem, seriously consider acquiring help from a psychologist or psychiatrist! If ultimately you are able to eliminate or partially correct even two or three (significant) imperfections,...you will be a much better man for it!

MAKE YOURSELF MORE APPEALING WITH A PHYSICAL AND SOCIAL MAKEOVER

This initiative is both easy and a complete *no brainer*. Surely, it is obvious, that if you improve your external (superficial) features from where they are now (and were during your marriage) to a new improved, healthier and better place, you will have a greater likelihood of reconciling with your ex-wife. There is definitely a reasonable possibility that she'll love the new you! Plus, you'll undoubtedly meet higher *quality* ladies in the interim! And, should this logic not be obvious, please read these chapters multiple times until you have completely embraced the concepts. Believe it or not, you have indirectly received a gift through the marital breakdown. You will have the opportunity to raise the level of your being, become a more desirable person and be more appreciated by those around you. Take it seriously; see it as a second *lease* on life, put in a genuine effort and you will be rewarded in ways you can't yet fathom!

Your ex-spouse has a precise image of you **exactly as you are today**. She sees you at best with the predominance of mediocrity and more likely as a guy with lots of baggage and negative qualities. But, that is easily changed! Think of yourself as an automobile. Most people would prefer a Mercedes over a Chevrolet? Both are shiny metal cars that get you from point 'A' to point 'B' quite nicely. But, the Mercedes is *top of the line* with the highest level of luxury and superior external looks while the Chevrolet represents the masses. And, guess what, it's easy to be *top of the line*!

For example, if you generally dress in blue jeans and a T-shirt, your attire can easily be elevated to a much trendier level. If you have poor hygiene, that can be improved as well. If your education is underwhelming, you can enroll in night courses. And, if you are overweight, that can be remedied too by way of a diet and exercise program. I am confident that you see where I'm going with this. Almost everything *superficial* can be altered and/or improved and much of it without costing a single cent. It merely takes a little effort and dedication. The choice is yours. But, I hope that you make the right one. Certainly, the likelihood of you reconciling with your ex is greatly enhanced if you undertake such improvements. So, stop dwelling on the past and start embracing your future.

OK, so you're not the best looking dude on the street. Well, most men aren't. Yet, I'm sure that you've seen lots of average looking guys accompanied by good looking ladies! Plus, your ex married you once, didn't she? So, you were attractive enough then. Plus, most women will take quality of other characteristics over good looks when they choose a guy to tie the knot! So, stop worrying about your facial features and concentrate on other areas that are easy to improve. If you upgrade yourself using just a small handful of the suggestions herein and rectify only one quarter of the things that disappointed your ex,...you will have effectively transformed yourself into an entirely new and visibly enhanced person,.....and one that is far more desirable than the last.

But, some effort is required as the changes you make must be both permanent and genuine or your ex won't be interested. I can however, guarantee that none of the effort nor the improvements will be wasted! All will be positive for you and everyone around you. Your life will be greatly improved and happier. And, so will the life of anyone you might choose to unite with.

To that end, here is a list of items that will be helpful in improving your external image. Seriously consider improving the ones most applicable and beneficial to you. Please take the time to read the list more than once and be honest with yourself. You don't need to do all the ones that might be applicable to you. But, you should definitely endeavor to do as many as possible. You might find it beneficial to recall the items that your ex-spouse might have considered disappointing! And, you are not seeking perfection,...only improvement. For example, if you are 100 pounds overweight, losing 25 pounds (and keeping it off) is a real and significant accomplishment!

- Do something extraordinary that might pique your ex-wives' interest. If you are balding,...consider a hair transplant. If you are a smoker,...give it up. You want to become a different more improved person than the one that she originally met, married...and *kicked* out!

- Get into shape so that you look better and feel better. If your body weight is excessive by 25 % or more lose half of the excess. In other words, if your height (6' 2") dictates that you should weigh 200-225 pounds, but, you actually weigh over 275 pounds, shed 25-30 pounds (half of the 50-60 excessive pounds).

- Use scented deodorant and a nice cologne. Don't buy a cheap brand of cologne.

- Shower daily and twice daily if you work out and/or sweat easily.

- Brush your teeth no less than 3 times daily and more often if possible. Leave a toothbrush and tooth paste at work AND in your car and use them. Use mouthwash frequently. Carry mints with you at all times (and take them when necessary). Nothing is more disgusting than bad breath.

- If your teeth are excessively yellow, consider getting them professionally whitened. Cigarette smoke and coffee are notorious for tooth yellowing and you should brush your teeth immediately after engaging or consuming either! Significantly yellowed teeth are not appealing to women (or anyone else). At minimum, use *over the counter* whitening compounds on a regular basis.

- Most women do not like excessive body hair. But, you are stuck with what you've got (unless you want to spend two hours a day shaving for the rest of your life). However, shave your private areas and keep the darned place squeaky clean at all times. It can never be too clean.

- Avoid garlic, onions and other smelly foods. Reduce your intake of any foods that activate unpleasant smells in your body especially 24 hours before a date. Broccoli, brussel sprouts, cabbage and asparagus are some of the worst foods for causing (ongoing) body odors. Even red meat, alcohol, beer, wine, and spicy foods cause some less than perfect body odors.

- Work out,...but, not to any extreme. Most women like to look at (and even date) pumped up muscular guys,...but, few actually marry them! One half hour to one hour work-outs three times a week is plenty. Spread the time evenly between stretching, cardio and upper and lower body exercises. Do this faithfully and you'll see great results in short order.

- Become more secure and LOOK IT! Walk *tall*. Stop slouching and work at improving your general posture. Stand tall and be tall.

- Upgrade your wardrobe. Don't wear blue jeans every day. And incinerate your track pants completely! In fact, wear pants that are slim, trim and fit! Contrary to popular belief, showing the crack of your ass is not appealing! Stop wearing sweat shirts, T-shirts and sleeveless shirts unless you live on the beach or are in the gym. Try to be more fashionable and introduce some class into your attire. STOP wearing track shoes and sneakers and start wearing dress shoes and upscale jackets. And, clean your shoes regularly.

- Ensure that you are well groomed and shaved every day. If you have un-kept facial hair,...shave it off or at minimum, keep it trimmed! After having my 'stache' for more than half my life, I toasted it for a good looking blonde who didn't like facial hair. Not a bad trade! However, a neatly trimmed short beard and moustache can also be attractive to women. If however, yours is grey,...not so much. Trim the hair in your ears and nose frequently. Clean your fingernails regularly and when they become dirty as well. Make a point of looking great all the time as you never know when you will meet or be in the company of a lady.

- Keep your car clean inside and out at all times. You never know when you might have a cute passenger.

- Keep your house or apartment clean at all times. There should be no dirty dishes in the sink, your bed should be made (every day) and dirty laundry should be in the hamper. Plus, your bathroom and particularly the toilet should be spotless at all times. Remember, you might be bringing someone home unexpectedly.

- If you are in the habit of being habitually late,...stop it. As I mentioned earlier, it is pure laziness and nobody likes it. Take pride in being on time and do whatever it takes to do so.

- If you don't already have a hobby,...get one. Women like guys who have other interests, speak other languages, cook and/or play music. There are an infinite number of other hobbies as well. So, it's easy to pick one that interests you and one that you'll stick with.

- Improve your social skills. Women don't like awkward guys. Buy a 'How To Master Social Skills' book if necessary. Your local book store sales person can assist you for sure.

- Stop swearing and use proper English. Take a course if necessary.

- Read a book and advance your knowledge. Go back to (night) school and take a course in English, another language, history, or any other **useful** topic that might make you smarter and/or better informed.

- Smile, try and be nicer and kinder to everyone around you and take the edge off. Be more sociable in general. For example, talk to the cleaning person or the security guard at your place of work. Start engaging and communicating with others. More importantly, allow the time for others to communicate with you! You'll find the *world* a much better place and easier to cope with!

- Don't take yourself too seriously. Stop being overly controlling and overbearing. Women aren't generally impressed with either characteristic. Be more human, receptive to the ideas of others and when appropriate a little playful.

- Be confident but lose the drama.
- Stop getting excited at every little thing. Try to maintain control (of yourself) at all times. If you can't keep your voice tone at one level, stop talking! In this case, "Silence is golden!"

- Stop complaining about everything and everyone. Don't criticize people (including your ex) and communicate in a positive fashion. Demonstrate empathy when someone is expressing a hardship that they are experiencing.

- STOP SMOKING,...it's a nasty, smelly habit that will kill you. Nobody likes it anymore and you'll live longer without it. At the very least cut down by a minimum of 50 % and only smoke when alone and outdoors. Brush your teeth or take a breath mint immediately thereafter. Use cologne after smoking,...EVERYWHERE, as the smoke makes clothing stink!

- Ease up on the alcohol a tad. Surprisingly, you can enjoy life much more with much less of that stuff. You will feel better, food will taste better and sex will definitely be better (because you won't be passing out or going to sleep prematurely).

- Be *better* than the guy your ex-wife met and fell in love with. Demonstrate manners and be more gentlemanly. It's NOT out of style!

- Engage in frequent visitations with your children and be very flexible if your ex-wife wants to make reasonable changes. Pick your kids up on time. Offer to pick them up at school and deliver them there as well if that is helpful. It will allow you to spend more time with them. It will also help the NO CONTACT rule (if you pick them up at school). Plus, most of these arrangements can be completed using texts which will also assist in maintaining the no contact rule.

Well, I'm sure that you now have a better perspective on yourself and some of your external and more superficial shortcomings. If you are, in any way, self-aware, none of these *less than perfect* imperfections should be a huge surprise. If you are not particularly self-aware, then you might be quite devastated at the moment. Get over it! The good news is that, with a little bit of *spit and polish* most of the above blemishes can be eradicated or significantly improved rather quickly! It merely takes a little dedication, effort and time. Keep in mind that the objective here is to legitimately and sincerely transform yourself into, not merely an improved person,....but one that your ex-wife might like to reconcile with!

WILL I "LOSE" MY EX WHILE I'M GETTING MY ACT IN GEAR?

Maybe, but, not likely,...especially within the first four to five months after you separated. Your ex-wife needs time to heal and regain her composure as well. Although she clearly knew that the separation was coming, her discontent, unhappiness and frustrations didn't vanish the day you separated. And getting her new life started (as you know) is challenging and stressful too. Plus, she needs time to reflect as well and, that reflection may well work to your benefit. So, unless she left you for another guy, it is unlikely that she's dating just yet.

However, your ex-spouse is similarly going to *head off* in search of a great new life with hopes of distancing herself from those feelings of disenchantment and disappointment. Eventually, she too might venture into dating as a distraction and confidence builder! Most likely, she will try and appease all the inadequacies and frustrations that she encountered (during the marriage) by finding a *better* more suitable man to create the new relationship of her dreams,....one that is superior (and 'greener') than the previous one.

Having said that, it never ceases to amaze me how many women actually believe that they can accomplish that massive undertaking (of acquiring a perfect life) in one small, easy step! Those are daunting tasks that are better suited to those with considerable time, youth and finances and are rarely achieved in their totality even then!

In addition, normal personal insecurities, that are common to everyone, seem to have a much larger impact as we get older and *things* start to fade. Age itself is a difficult phenomenon with which to reconcile, especially for women. Accordingly, as separated women look for the perfect new life and partner, it is commonly not without some regret for leaving their past life. Plus, they frequently find the new road difficult and bumpy with few guarantees along the way and no "Hollywood" successes stories at its end. And, many reminisce that they once possessed much of what they are currently seeking!

So, it's important to give your ex-wife the time and *rope* to go through this process. New relationship success is not necessarily going to be part of her future *story* and you don't want any connection or association should she fail. That will only reinforce the same negative feelings that prompted her to separate from you in the first place. So, keep your distance. Also, keep in mind that although your ex-wife's' current perception of you and the marriage likely remains unreasonably negative,.....it is VERY, VERY real to her! So, don't give her any additional reason or ammunition to hang onto those misconceptions. You want to remain completely absent from her new life so that the reality of her actions and fate have the opportunity to play out! As I mentioned above, it will likely be a frustrating path, sprinkled with disappointment and after a period of time she might well realize that the *grass* in your backyard was not so bad at all! That's when she'll be more receptive to getting together and/or talking.

Surprisingly, your ex might well reach out to you in the early days, weeks and months following the separation. But, don't be confused by those calls. THOSE CALLS will undoubtedly be for assistance on items with which she is experiencing problems. Those calls will likely be for pure self-serving reasons,...so that she can effectively have her cake (namely all the things that she wants to retain from the marriage),...and the icing too (the separation). Try and avoid her out-reach (for assistance) without appearing overly insensitive. The sooner that you are able to truly sever the relationship and enter the NO CONTACT zone, the sooner the program for possible reunification can begin. Do NOT communicate or engage her (unless absolutely necessary) for a minimum of four months. Do not enable her for the same period. It will not benefit you in terms of your goal to reunite.

So, warm up to the fact that, at some point, your wife is going to date or will quickly move in with her lover. That will hurt a lot! But, resist all urges to react in a manner which is immature, illegal or demeaning to yourself. Don't drive to her house and make a scene. Don't text offensive messages or otherwise engage in name calling. Try to rise above that petty stuff at this painful juncture. Your ability to retain a nonchalant attitude will likely reap huge benefits later. Either your ex will see a stronger, more mature and more appealing 'you' (and want to rekindle something) or she will stay her course and you will already have adopted characteristics that will be very appealing to the next lady! It's a *win win* situation. Plus, rebound relationships rarely go the distance. And, if you create a new and improved 'you', your wife's other dates will become little more than comparative *material*,...something that may also work to your benefit. In summation, try to emulate the three Musketeers,...and be strong, steadfast and cavalier!

During the first four months (following your separation) and as I mentioned earlier, I STRONGLY urge you to move on with your life IMMEDIATELY and assume that your wife is not coming back. I say that for three reasons. Firstly and most obviously, she might not come back. There's no guarantee of her returning even if she does *wake up* to a more reasonable sense of reality. Plus, she might get incredibly lucky and actually find greener pastures in relative short order. You want to have at least started your own new life should that happen. There is NO mileage whatsoever in wasting another six months of your life waiting (for her) when you could be better utilizing that time to heal, regroup and potentially meet someone better suited! Finally, by dating, you might meet someone better and more complimentary to your character.

As I've suggested before, if at any time your ex wants to reverse things, you are far better off to be in a confident position of strength wherein you will be able to make a more balanced decision. Waiting will only add to your vulnerability and will NOT assist you in getting back together. In fact, your ex will not warm up to a sign of weakness. She can tolerate your dating much easier! Keep in mind that time isn't necessarily on your side either (although it is more frequently harsher for women), so best you *waste* as little as possible!

Some ex-spouses will be very unpleasant, harsh, acrimonious and even vicious during and after separation. They will test your resolve as a matter of course and they will do so relentlessly. These specific women will be difficult at every *turn* from the moment you separate and indefinitely into the future. They will go out of their way to infuriate and upset you. The reasons for their bitterness and vengeful behavior are simple enough (at least to them). Firstly, they attribute the marital failure and breakdown entirely to you. Plus, they see you as having completely wasted a big part of their life. Accordingly, they will go to great lengths to ensure your unhappiness wherein no act of retribution will be *out of bounds*! Even though they gave you walking papers, they have no desire to see you improving your lot. Many will endeavor to manipulate your children and commit many of the mistakes that I specifically counseled you (earlier) to avoid. With an ex like that, it will be a trying time for sure.

I recall one incident (of many) when I was picking up my daughter from school on a Friday afternoon, as I had on many Fridays before. It was to be my *every other weekend* visitation and naturally I was there on time to receive her. However, on this occasion the school authorities declined to turn her over stating that her mother had called earlier and advised that I had no visitation or weekend custody rights. I was always wise enough to keep a copy of the court sanctioned custody papers on hand whenever I was in the presence of my children. So, I showed the papers to the school principal and advised them (discreetly and quietly) that if my daughter was not released to my custody, I would involve the police department. They promptly delivered my daughter to my charge.

If you have been married to a person such as the one that I have just described, I question whether this is someone that you really would want to win back as the chances of an acrimonious reunion would be high. Moreover, this person is not ready to forgive you and you should consider the possibility that she might never be ready!

WHAT CAN I EXPECT IF I'M THE ONE WHO WAS CHEATING,... AND GOT CAUGHT?

Now, I know that you've been wondering whether your impropriety has created an irreversible situation in as far as your marriage and possible reconciliation. So, I best tell you now to, sit down, take a deep breath, put your head between your legs and kiss your sorry *butt* (and your wife) goodbye! LOL Oh my goodness,...I had to say it. It's not my joke, but, it *gets me going* every time! Sorry.

In all seriousness though,.....**NO**, believe it or not, your relationship is not necessarily over even if you were the moron caught 'screw-in' around! It certainly doesn't help that you cheated, but, it is not over just yet.

Divorce Magazine suggests that 70% of couples actually stay together (and/or get back together) after one or the other admits to an affair! In other words, while 30% of marriages with an unfaithful spouse end in divorce, the vast majority seem to work things out. Interestingly, men who cheat almost never marry the woman with whom they had a discreet liaison. In fact, I do not know of one such individual! And, that actually supports the notion that *mini-me* is steering the boat for many men and not your true emotional self.

Women, on the other hand, can act differently. I know of several ladies who had flings and did not marry the guys involved. However, I also know of several women who had clandestine relationships during their marriage and ultimately did marry their adulterous partners.

In summary, the possibilities for reconciling after **you** have had an affair are actually rather reasonable. But, it certainly won't be an easy road and justifiably so. Your wife has been hurt rather severely. She is devastated, angry and disenchanted at her core. And, she no longer trusts you,....not "as far as she could throw you." You have replaced whatever positive feelings she had regarding you, with feelings of distrust, disappointment and despair.

So, your journey will be fraught with bumps, curves and road blocks with your wife likely experiencing a wide range of often volatile emotions. Expect set-backs, rehashing of things seemingly already settled (at least in your mind), reopening of old wounds and endless repetition of the same question. WHY? So, if you truly want to rebuild your marriage, prepare yourself with the answer to that question! And, ensure that the answer has some merit, comes from your heart and lays you bare to any response whatsoever! Assuming that you are currently separated, complete everything from Step 1 to 4 in its entirety. Then follow the additional guidelines in the latter portion of Step 4 under "WHAT TO DO IF YOU CHEATED."

STEP 4 - TIME TO TEST THE 'WATERS' AND ARRANGE A COUPLE OF *CHANCE* ENCOUNTERS

Well, I am hopeful that you successfully completed the most important part of your trek towards recovery and reconciliation with your spouse. In summary, that means that you have allowed a minimum 4 month cooling down period during which you had no (or significantly limited) communication and/or interaction with your ex (except as might have been necessary for your children). In effect, you were entirely out of her life in every way over that period. During that time you undertook a variety of diversionary activities, including dating as a means of healing from the traumatic loss (of your wife) and in order to regain your confidence. You went out with no less than two different women and enjoyed a minimum of 8 dates (total). You took time to improve your appearance and you raised your level of ethics and morality thereby boosting your self-esteem even more. In addition, you took serious and honest 'stock' of the mistakes that you made during the marriage as well as the character flaws that contributed to those mistakes so that you could repent, change and ensure that the same mistakes are never made again. Essentially you created new *life* rules and guidelines (for yourself) so that you became a better person.

You also made regular financial arrangements for your wife (and children) and sought proper advice and direction from a lawyer. Finally, if you were the one caught cheating in your marriage, you spent additional time reflecting on that specific transgression and how to address it (see chapter "What To Do If I Cheated"). In essence, you sincerely believe that you have recovered from your loss and are now 100 %. You have also made yourself a better and stronger person and you have come to the realization that, should you not reunite with your ex-spouse, there are plenty of "fish in the sea" and you will be fine in your new life!

If you have not accomplished all of the above, I strongly urge you to take whatever additional time is necessary to complete the program effectively. To that end I vehemently advise you **not** to proceed until you are ready. If you do, things might start well enough as your ex-wife most likely hasn't been living her new life as a movie star and she might even miss you as well. But, your program will quickly go off the rails when she realizes, that you haven't changed (sufficiently) at all!

There is also the possibility that your ex-wife is not ready to even consider the thought of reconciliation. Look for the signs and try to be unbiased. For example, your ex is not ready if she continues to exhibit any of the following types of behavior.

- harsh reactions to anything you say or do

- raises your screw-ups from the marriage (directly or through your children)

- plays *head-games* regarding access to your children

- tends to be sarcastic during simple text/email exchanges

- lashes out by phone, text or email without current justification

Should any of these signs remain present, do not proceed with Step 4 until they have largely disappeared. As there is no guarantee that such a time will ever come, continue dating and seriously consider your other options.

That brings me to one more very important topic. While your ex might well have been the one initiating the separation, be absolutely positive that *you* want to reconcile. Make sure that your intentions are sincere and genuine and not the result of ego or a 'knee-jerk' response to return to status quo. You really have to be honest with yourself here. And, the idea that your kids are the justification for such action is both short sighted and NOT in their best interests at all. This is all about you and *you* must really want this or it will fail again and then your kids will experience the emotional roller coaster and stress all over again!

So, it's time for **you** to consider for a moment all the things that **you** didn't like about your marriage and your ex,...things that will more than likely continue unchanged (should you reconcile and) in spite of the new 'you!' Create a list of all those bothersome marital items that frustrated you during the marriage. Don't be petty. But, definitely list things that you prefer to live without! And, put notations alongside that speak to the likelihood (or lack thereof) that they might improve or abate after getting back together. Add to your list any negative aspects related to your ex-wife's character as well. Those annoyances are also likely to continue unchanged after any reconciliation. Then note how each one of these bothersome marital items or character annoyances might frustrate you (on a scale of 1 to 5) should you reconcile.

I had one ex-wife that had booze and illicit drug problems. And, naturally she dumped me! Needless to say, after I healed and regained my confidence,...I ran for the hills when her phone call came!

Compile another (second) list containing all the reasons why you cherish the marriage, want to reconcile and love your wife. This second list can contain your children as one item. But, if there are **less than** nine other positive and real reasons to reconcile (for a total of 10), you should really consider the possibility of **not** reuniting, especially if the first list (of things that frustrated you during the marriage) contains daunting results. Keep in mind that things like "I can't live without her" and "she's the only one for me" are more *fluff* than credible reasons to reconcile. First and foremost, those endearing but hollow comments probably represent more of a nervous reaction to having your life turned upside down by separating. In fact, if you are even thinking along the exclusive lines of, "I just love her so much", you have probably not completed the healing process as yet!

For example, (just prior to separating) did you look forward to and enjoy coming home from work to your spouse? Or did you linger and feel no compunction about entertaining (yourself) with after work activities to avoid going home whenever possible? Did your ex support your endeavors? Was the sex good? Was the marriage peaceful? Was your spouse a great homemaker? Could you rely on her? You want to list the *real* underlying reasons that you love your wife and want to reconcile!

Upon completion of these two lists you want to spend some considerable time reviewing and analyzing them. The process may not be easy. Or it might well be an eye opener! The point is to do some real soul searching before you make any further efforts towards reuniting so that you make the correct decision.

So, if you remain steadfast in wanting to win your ex back and if you have undertaken and completed the whole program thus far, you are likely looking good, feeling good and ready. Your confidence level is back to normal (and probably beyond) and you are effectively a new man! And, since you haven't put down this book and called one of your new girlfriends, let's go and get your ex!

This final stage of the program might be a tad tricky for some, at least at the beginning because you don't want to approach your ex directly just yet. **The intent here is to *perform* some subliminal advertising of the new and improved 'you' and simultaneously demonstrate that you are a changed and upgraded version of your former self.** This will be done over the course of 3 to 4 *chance* and seemingly random interactions. So, it must be a carefully orchestrated process,...one that does not appear contrived if possible. Accordingly, under no circumstances should you call and suggest that you want to meet for that very first interaction (post separation). By doing so you might appear weak and the plan will work better if you are in a position of strength,...**where she wants to get back together with you!** Worse, there's a certain amount of vulnerability if she declines and you don't want to have to go through a second rejection if avoidable! Even though you have fully recuperated and accept the possibility that you might not get her back, it is best not to tip your hand as yet. A much better option is a series of prearranged *happen-stance* encounters where you appear aloof and not really interested in reconciliation.

If your ex demonstrates some kind of suggestive sign that she might be ready for interaction, your path forward is a little easier. Understand that these *signs* are not necessarily conscious on her part and are more likely to be passive in nature. However, whether they are or are not overt, they do provide a suitable setting for your next move. Here are a few of the signs that indicate that the timing is appropriate for your first (post separation) encounter.

- She calls you after a considerable period of no contact. The reason for the call is irrelevant especially if she has not reached out prior.

- She enquires about you through a third party (friend, relative, etc.).

- You notice a positive change in your ex-wife's behavior towards you. After some women *throw* their spouses out, they become quite belligerent towards their ex-husbands both directly and indirectly. They sometimes become combative in no short amount! If these are your circumstances and you are also one of those ex-dads who must maintain some communication for the benefit of children, you might notice a positive change in her attitude at some point.

- She breaks up with her lover or boyfriend.

- You are picking up your children and you notice that she is coming out to the car (with them) more frequently than prior. Make sure that you are well dressed and in *tip top* shape should this happen.

- She delivers the children to your doorstep when she did not do so prior and it is not necessary. Once again, make sure that you are well dressed and in *tip top* shape should this happen.

- Your children tell you that mommy has been crying a lot! Resist the urge to engage them further. The information in and of itself is indicative. It is very important not to put children in the middle of a marital break-up, separation and/or dispute.

- You legitimately *cross paths* by accident and she engages you in conversation.

Any of the above signs of interest provide a good opportunity to set the stage for a first real (post separation) interaction between the two of you. So, provided that you've completed the first three steps herein, build upon any of the above opportunities that might present themselves. However, provided that your ex is not currently belligerent towards you, it is also acceptable to move forward without any obvious sign of her receptiveness.

It is now time to arrange that very first staged interaction where you can properly begin *selling* the new 'you!' It is important therefore, that you set up an *accidental* way to *cross paths* with your ex-wife. This first interaction should be just a brief, two minute SEE HER, HAVE A BRIEF CHAT and GO. When you do see her after the protracted period, you want to be well dressed, nicely groomed and look *hot as hell*. If you have a new car, try and park it in a visible location. Better still, arrange for a date to be waiting inside. If staged properly, that would be the perfect *hook*. To be clear, this part of the process is about advertising and fishing! You are advertising the new, improved and changed 'you' and you are *fishing* to see what feelings and emotions might surface from your ex. There is no question that you will re-ignite something. So, you want to show a genuine sincerity and happiness that you are chatting, but, with a degree of aloofness that leaves her wondering whether **YOU** still have any interest (or not)! Here are some interesting ways that you might discreetly arrange a brief first encounter.

- A good opportunity might be to pick up your kids early. On this occasion, get out of the car and ring the doorbell as you definitely want to be seen.

- Hang out at her local coffee bar at a time when you think that she might come in.

- Maybe you have an item of hers (like clothes, books, music, etc.,) that you *think* she might want. Text her and suggest that you were throwing some things out, came across this item and was wondering if she wants it!

- Maybe you want something from her (like clothes, books,

music, etc.,). In this case, you can ask for it by text and then, of course, pick it up.

- As you are likely providing support checks, you could arrange (at the outset) to have then run out after six months and then use that opportunity to meet.

- Maybe you can text your wife that your vehicle has a flat and you can't bring the kids home. Make sure that you sound very apologetic and don't involve your kids in the 'charade.' Ask if she might mind picking them up. And, make sure your vehicle remains out of site!

If none of these suggestions for a first interaction fit your circumstances, figure out and try something that does. Just be cognizant that it needs to appear as a natural, casual and unintended encounter. Whatever your choice for this *accidental* first crossing, keep interaction short and upbeat. A quick "Hi there, it's really nice to see you", with all the confidence that you can muster, will be perfect. Maintain an aloof but friendly presence. You definitely want to engage,...but, not too much. You want to inadvertently *show off* the new upgraded version of 'you' as well as find out a bit about her (new existence). Ask her how she is making out and "what is new in her life?" She might ask you the same. **So, be prepared with interesting responses,...something that might intrigue her.** For example, "I've taken up skiing" or "I've been going to cooking classes",....anything out of the ordinary in terms of your former marriage. Keep an eye on her reactions as that will be a tell-tale sign for initiating the next encounter. Hopefully, you will see some sign of interest even if it is just a casual sign.

But, don't rush this stage, or it might well backfire. In fact, following the first encounter, you need to arrange two or three more of these brief, accidental *advertising* sessions over (no less than) a one month period. Each time you must be well dressed, standing *tall*, confident and looking good. With luck the encounters will get a little longer and more engaging each time. In reality, you are forming a new *friendship* and one that your ex might genuinely be inclined to enjoy. Slowly, she might divulge certain personal information that could conceivably shed more light on her situation and intentions. The objective is to listen and gage how happy she might be in her *new* life,...or not. No matter what she says, acknowledge positively, with real empathy and display the new 'you',...a compassionate and considerate 'you.' Inevitably, she will be even more trusting and, as such, more forthcoming with the things that are really going on in her life. For example, she might tell you if she is dating and/or if there is a (new) beau in her life or not. Every bit of information that you can extract from her will assist you in planning your next move.

As I mentioned, after the first *accidental* encounter, you want to arrange two or three more brief and preferably *chance* interactions over (approximately) a one month period. If it becomes difficult to orchestrate, come up with semi-legitimate reasons (**other** than the topic of your marriage) to see her. Maybe there is a document (for taxes) that one of you needs. Just create a seemingly legitimate reason to meet. At this stage, if your wife's disposition is relaxed and receptive, it does not really matter if your efforts appear a tad contrived. If, on the other hand, she is not interested, she'll let you know by not playing along. However, if the new 'you' has rekindled even some interest, she'll undoubtedly want to confirm whether it's real or not! But, do NOT call her,....rather (if you can't arrange something that appears accidental), send her a brief text relating your desire to meet (and why). You want to appear low key and casual in your approach. In fact, **you** want to appear somewhat DISINTERESTED (especially in regards to getting back together)! So, no phone calls.

As one or both of the next 2 or 3 interactions might need to be orchestrated more overtly, arrange to meet (if possible) at a place of her choosing. Try to finesse at least one meeting around the dinner hour (between 5:00 and 6:00 pm) and preferably on a

Saturday night so that you can give the impression that you've got a date thereafter. You might be going out with the guys, but she won't know the difference. You want to keep her interested and guessing at this stage. When you do see her, keep the meeting relatively short. But, you want to be in TOP FORM. That means, well dressed, nicely groomed and most of all appear HAPPY, BUSY and CONFIDENT. You MUST appear cheerful, on top of your *game* and generally thrilled with your new life. Use your best manners and project the new and improved *you*.

Once again (and on one of the 2 or 3 interactions), you want to appear to be in a bit of a hurry (as if you are on a tight schedule). Should she ask, be honest and say that you have plans. If you **do** have a date, you ***can*** casually slip that in. Say something like, "I can't chat for too long as I have early plans with someone." In other words, infer that you are going out on a date by being sparse with the details! But, under no circumstances should you lie. Also, on each of these occasions, try and (briefly) mention one of the new hobbies that you are pursuing, trips that you have or might be taking, new interests, etc.,…anything that might be considered out of the ordinary during your marriage.

At one of my semi-contrived encounters (I think the third or fourth), I choreographed things so that my date answered the door when I knew that my ex was coming to pick up school books that the kids had *accidently* left behind. Then, I went outside (closed the door behind myself) and engaged in a nice conversation with her for ten minutes. That was the "hook" for sure in my situation. Human beings are incredibly predictable when it involves wanting something (or someone) that they seemingly can't have! Think about Adam and Eve and the proverbial *apple*.

These little charades are "tried and true" and will slowly get your ex-wife thinking. Hopefully, her thoughts will be positive, more about the new and improved 'you' and less about your *old* failings. If you have done your homework properly, she now sees an interesting upgraded version of the man she once fell in love with! But, don't *blow* it with inappropriate comments. No matter what the current realities, **never say anything negative about her, or her boyfriend, or anything else whatsoever.**

You want to remain upbeat, positive, in control and gentlemanly. Stay strong and rise above that petty stuff. You are now much *better* than the old *you*. No longer do insecurities, an inflated ego and/or bad habits drag you down! If you can remain positive, confident, and cordial through each of the three or four encounters, your chances of success are optimal. As each meeting ends, she will invariably think back about the early years with you and all the good times that you two enjoyed. Even if she, herself is dating and/or living with another man, she will be bothered by the thought that some other lady might get what she let go! And, when she compares you to her 'new' but, likely imperfect (rebound) fellow, you might well edge him out. In fact, **you** might indeed get a phone call! However, that call will never come and this process will never work if you try to short circuit the program or you revert to your old ways. Time MUST pass and for good reason. It affords the opportunity to form a new relationship based upon your new (and better) self. Plus, the old adage that *time makes the heart grow fonder*, is very real! So, don't be overly anxious, keep your cool, make the new upgraded 'you' a permanent reality and continue the steps (outlined herein) to the end.

IT'S TIME TO *DIRECTLY* ASK YOUR EX TO MEET,...
IT'S TIME TO SAY YOU'RE SORRY!

If all of the 3 or 4 *chance* encounters went reasonably well or at least without incident then it is finally time to overtly ask your ex-wife to meet for a more heart to heart get together. This is not the same as one of the previous accidental encounters. So, it's not the time for a casual text or an E-mail. This is the time for something more endearing and mood setting. This is the time for an old fashioned letter that is hand written. It will be short,...but, it's going to be a *tear jerker* for sure! And, you will finally get to ask the question for which you have been preparing for months.

So, purchase a friendship card,...preferably one that costs more than a dollar and does **not** have the words "I love you" splashed all over it. Then, with a normal pen and in your own handwriting write your ex-wife a sincere letter that **APPLIES TO YOUR INDIVIDUAL CIRCUMSTANCES.** Consider first writing a draft on a separate piece of paper so that you get the content just right. You are writing a heartfelt and sincere apology for causing the marital breakdown. It should express your sorrow for having hurt her in the process. And, it should contain a brief summary of the changes that you've made as the result. **Do not use the words, "I love you" and do not tell her that you want to get back together.** But, include a clear expression of sincere feelings about your responsibilities (for the break-up) and your remorse. Your card might read something like the following (**but please put this into your own words**).

- "I know that it must have been very hard for you to initiate the separation and I should have written this note months ago,...but, I was dealing with losing you and a little messed up at that time. I now understand how badly I screwed up and why you decided to leave and I accept your decision."

- "I truly apologize for all the pain, grief and stress that I clearly caused you. I was an incredible jerk and a obvious failure as a husband. I don't know why you put up with me as long as you did? After we separated, I did some real soul searching, went for counseling and worked on several of my major issues and shortcomings. I think that I've actually made some good headway. I am no longer "***as controlling as I was***" or "***I don't drink anymore***" or "***I cut off the affair immediately after we separated when I realized that I had lost everything that I really wanted.*** " (you fill in the appropriate improvements that you actually made)

- "Anyway, I honestly hope that things have improved for you because I truly want the best for you,...even if I didn't show it during the marriage. I really regret the outcome. I do hope that you are feeling better. I'm feeling a little better too. In fact, I'm thinking about going away for a while and thought that we might get together before I do so. Is there a chance that you'd meet for a coffee or dinner? Just drop me a text when it's convenient."

That's it,...relatively **short** and sweet. No, "I love you." No, "I miss you." No sweet nothings at all! This is a 'hook' and nothing more. You are fishing to see whether she might still have feelings for you,...enough to consider a reconciliation. And, DON'T CALL IT A DATE. You want her to think that **YOU** believe the relationship to be over and as the result, might be moving on,....and **YOU ARE** if she doesn't *bite*! Drop the card in the mail and hang on. If you don't hear back within the next seven days, text a simple note. "Did you get my card? Are you able to meet?" Don't say another word. The rest is up to her and fate.

If you played your *cards* correctly right up to this point, your ex is going to have a real cry as she reads your card,...even if her lover is in the next room! In any case, this will be the moment of truth. If she says "yes", you are "made in the shade" and it is all yours (not) to *screw up* again!

SHE SAID "YES" TO MEETING ME,....
AM I ON THE ROAD TO RECONCILIATION?

Yes, but, you are not quite all the way there just yet. EVERYTHING now *rides* on the outcome of your first real and unfeigned get-together. But, you need to prepare once again.

Firstly, you want to choose a quiet venue where you can talk and be heard easily by each other. So, don't choose a place with loud music or where the tables are so close that you'll be having a *group* discussion with other guests. If she is amiable to meeting for dinner, pick a nice place that **you** have been to before. The idea is that **you** are in familiar and comfortable surroundings so that there are no unexpected occurrences. But, don't pick a place where you and your ex enjoyed dinner when you were together. You want her to be motivated but still *guessing* a tad. Plus, you want to protect yourself should things not go in the direction that you would like. Make a reservation. Then text your ex-wife with the location, date and time and ask her nicely if she could meet you there. Do **NOT** offer to pick her up. Keep things casual for a tad while longer. Plus, if things go *south*, you'll want to have a timely and simple exit plan that doesn't involve you taking her home! But, don't appear or sound *cold* or impersonal. You want your text to be brief but congenial. You can close with "Looking forward to seeing you." And, try and accommodate any of her (response) wishes no matter what they might be. Then start to prepare for what you will say.

Your *dinner* **SPEECH** should involve four distinct segments which are explained below. I would suggest that you write out your intended oral dissertation with particular emphasis around aspects B, C and D. Don't take a chance on *winging it*. You have all the time in the world to organize your thoughts beforehand so that the ultimate delivery is sincere, believable and accomplishes the task. And, to ensure that everything stays on track, memorize your speech and stick to the script that you prepare. **Don't stray from it at all**. Your speech (and as such your preparation) should contain:

A) The **Greeting**, B) The **Apology**, C) The **Changes that you've made** and how you've become a better person and D) The **Close**.

A) THE GREETING

The initial (face to face) greeting should be warm and gracious and maybe even involve a brief hug if you are comfortable doing so and your ex is into that sort of thing (and most women are). Make sure that you are well groomed and well dressed. Wear new shoes and new clothes,...something that she has not seen you in prior (and NO RUNNING SHOES, SANDALS, TRACK PANTS, T-SHIRTS or BACK PACKS). Spend some money on your attire for this meeting because if you *blow it*, you won't likely have another chance! Put new cologne on as well and not the cheap stuff either! Make sure that it smells expensive and buy something that you did not use during the marriage. Make sure that you don't splash it all over.

You want the overall effect to be subtle and aloof,...but, not over the top! You want an image that says,...*yes, I'm well-dressed now and wearing expensive cologne, but, not specifically for you. This is merely the new me!* If you had a habit of being late when you were married, make sure that you are on time for this get-together. But, try and arrive a minute or two after she does and preferably once she is already seated. **Tell her how great she looks immediately upon seeing her and BEFORE she has time to say anything to you.**

B) THE APOLOGY

After getting settled and exchanging a few pleasantries, compliment her again. Say something like, **"Gee, did you do something different with your hair,...it looks great**!" Continue the *small talk* until you have ordered drinks and dinner. You don't want to be excessively interrupted for the next part. Then, you can begin with a heartfelt apology that is delivered in much greater detail then you did in your (mailed) card. Here are some of the things that should be covered. You want to express four distinct points; i) The mistakes that you made during the marriage, ii) How unreasonable your behavior was, iii) How much you hurt your wife unnecessarily and through NO fault of hers and iv) How sorry you are for doing so and how much you regret splitting up. You MUST provide all the *gory* details. It is completely unacceptable to make general statements that do not delineate the specifics of **your** situation and **your** **screw-ups**. Here are a few possible examples that might be helpful. Each one, more or less, embodies all four points.

- I was incredibly insecure, ridiculously jealous and acted like a child. I can't believe how off-side I was. I caused you so much pain and grief. I was so wrapped up in my own insecurities, that I completely lost sight of the person that meant the most to me. I can't tell you how truly sorry I am. Splitting up was the absolute worst day of my life.

- I should not have been so overbearing and aggressive towards you. I was completely self-centered and out of line. I didn't mean to make you so unhappy. Much more of our relationship should have been about you and not me. I can't believe that I blew the best chance in my life to have someone like you.

- I was thoughtless and complacent and shouldn't have been so wrapped up in sports (or work or video games or TV). I should have spent much more time with you. I was consumed with the wrong things and had no idea how much I was hurting you. I am sincerely sorry for disappointing you and ruining our marriage. I just wish that I could go back in time and do it again. I would not be such a screw-up again!

- I am incredibly sorry that I cheated. I was in a vulnerable state with more stress than I could handle and I lost control. She never meant anything to me. I was so in love with you. I can't believe how I screwed up! But, I got caught in a weak moment and it only happened once. I didn't mean to hurt you like that and am really sorry. What an ignorant thing for me to do. I disappointed the one person that I care about most. It was stupid and I have never regretted anything more in my life. (See also "WHAT TO DO IF YOU CHEATED" below)

- I was thoughtless and self-centered. It was wrong of me to *dump* all the responsibility of the marriage (and the children) on you. I should have acted like an adult and handled my fair share. Instead, I stressed you out and made you unhappy. I can't believe that I was so insensitive to the one that mattered the most. I am really sorry for all the anguish and unhappiness that I caused you. The day we separated was the worst day of my life.

- I was completely insensitive and unsympathetic when you talked about things that bothered you (like your job) and really should have been more supportive. Instead of thinking about you I was preoccupied with myself. I am sorry for being such a jerk. I can't believe that I hurt you so much. Splitting up with you made me realize just how bad a husband I really was.

Finally, you must advise your ex that you have taken 'stock' and done some real soul searching to address your failings. Hopefully, you can legitimately add that you sought therapy and it helped (but, only if you did). If your ex suggests that she might have been complicit in the marital problems, simply say, "Maybe,...but, I was the bigger culprit for sure."

Don't let the conversation switch to her involvement in the break-up. It usually doesn't end well. If the discussion does go in that direction, don't interrupt or try to control her comments. Be respectful and let her finish. Then tell her that if you had not acted so poorly in most respects, you would probably still be together.

There is a balance here as far as the delivery. You want to appear very genuine and truly sorry but not so *gooey* that you start crying before she does! Red eyes would be perfect! Try and act as naturally as possible, be compassionate and end with another apology.

C) THE CHANGES

You claimed that you've changed and have become a better person! Great,...now prove it. Those are easy words to say. In fact, I just wrote them here in a split second and with little effort. So, as they say in business, "show me the money." In no uncertain terms you need to provide credible back-up and proof of your claims that you've really changed and have become a better person. It is paramount that you outline all the major changes that you assert to have made as well as the details (hopefully) that corroborate the positive results. And, how do you do that? Well, you don't whine and you don't repeat the following silly (unsubstantiated) comment ten times; "I've changed", "I've changed",..."I've really changed." You provide some kind of accreditation and evidence that backs up your assertions. For example:

- Tell your ex-wife about some of your experiences at AA (Alcoholics Anonymous).

- Share with your wife some of the details regarding the exercises that your therapist has given you to alter and reduce your temper.

- Advise your wife that in your soul searching you highlighted 5 terrible shortcomings that you have and you created little exercises and programs to improve them. Tell her that you practice every day and show her one of your work sheets!

- Advise your ex of the volunteer work that you are doing and how it has given you a different and more empathetic perspective on those around you. Tell her where you are doing the work and describe it to her.

It is critical that your ex believes everything that you are telling her and beyond a reasonable doubt. Remember also that her close friends and close confidents will be more critical of your apparent new convictions! If your ex-wife doesn't believe your claims,...you are going to be *toast*. And, if she thinks that you're lying,....you're going to be 'burnt toast!' So, think this part of the process through carefully long before your important little rendezvous. Don't think for a moment that you can deliver this "off the cuff" and expect to accomplish your goals. You are very close now, so, do this properly, write it out (point form would be suggested), memorize it and stick to your script.

D) **THE CLOSE**
This is the ultimate "moment of truth." The finale! Everything that you've worked so hard to achieve will be put to the test in a few brief minutes. Your approach is critical but relatively straight forward,......a summary of the mistakes you've made and the remorse that you feel, followed **NOW** by the words, **"I STILL LOVE YOU"** and the question that you've been waiting to ask for months.

"WOULD YOU CONSIDER GETTING BACK TOGETHER?"

Although the CLOSE is short, there is still merit in your preparing for the *conclusion* as this is not the time to mess things up through laziness or oversight. With luck, it will be the time when your marital demise begins to reverse direction!

Here is a recap of the "SHE SAID 'YES' TO MEETING ME" section. Make sure that you write out in detail everything that you intend to say in advance and memorize it thoroughly. You can't over-prepare! Then, and only then, proceed as follows.

- Ensure that you **dress to kill** and be on time for your get-together.

- Take tissues as someone is going to need them!

- **Greet her with a compliment** and exchange some pleasantries.

- Order your dinner so that your speech has few interruptions.

- **Detail all of the various mistakes that you committed** during the marriage (and that caused and/or contributed to the breakup). Elaborate on your unreasonable behavior and how it caused the demise as well. **Be specific and genuine**!

- Articulate that you now know how much you hurt your wife and take full responsibility for the outcome. Express heartfelt regret for the large amount of pain and suffering that you and your deplorable conduct have caused your wife. **Be sincere**.

- Relate to her that you **did not appreciate the consequences** of your actions (or inactions) at the time and the revelation has caused you great sorrow.

- Emphasize how much you **regret splitting up** and make clear that **responsibility for the separation rests entirely on your shoulders.**

- **Apologize for your flaws, your mistakes and all the pain and suffering that you caused your ex.**

- **Delineate all the changes that you've made and provide evidence of same**. The more credibility that you can provide, the more believable this will be!

- No matter your wife's comments to any of the above, **you will not respond with anything negative, sarcastic or unrehearsed. STICK TO YOUR SCRIPT.**

And, finally, your closing remarks should probably go something like this:

- "**I only wish that there was some way that I could change the past.** But, there's not,...I can only change the future. I feel that

I've come a long way and know that I wouldn't make the same mistakes again. I'd be much more supportive by (*fill in the blanks*) _____, _____ and _____".

- Plus, say "I'd be prepared to do anything else that you might want because I still love you."

- "I don't honestly expect you to simply reverse your decision in a heartbeat. You had a real loser for a spouse, and you did the right thing by separating. **But, maybe we could slowly start again and you could see just how much I've really changed.** I'd genuinely like to be the husband that you deserve in a future relationship. I'd like you to consider working towards reconciliation. Maybe we could date for a while or seek counseling together or both. Would you think about it?"

Then, you STOP TALKING entirely. Don't babble and don't beg. DON'T SAY ANYTHING.

Simply wait for her answer. It's now up to your ex to play the next card. She may start crying, she may answer "yes" (in the moment), she may ask for time to think about it, she might say "no" and she might even give you *hell* for causing this unfortunate mess in the first place. If she gets upset and/or argumentative, do NOT engage her. **ACCEPT** whatever she says completely. Acknowledge her response appropriately even if she says "no." **Don't go off the deep end!** Remember, you are supposed to be an improved and better person. Hold your composure and simply respond, **"Thank you for at least listening and considering my request."**

To reiterate, if things don't go quite the way you would like, act like a responsible caring adult. If the answer is a resounding "no",....don't object, don't complain and don't plead. I have advised above how to respond, but here it is again. **"Thank you for at least listening and considering my request."** Once again and in the case of a "no" answer, do **NOT** try and change her mind under any circumstances because you will only lessen the effect of your pitch.

In reality and no matter what she answers, she will be thinking about your *sermon* intensely over the next few days and probably much longer! **So, even an initial "no" can easily become a future "yes!"** Accordingly, keep things friendly and as upbeat as possible for the rest of the evening. Trust me, if you played all your cards right, she's feeling sorry for you now. So, don't blow it! Console her with tissues as might be appropriate. You'll get points for that! Use one yourself if necessary. You'll get even more points for that! After things calm down a bit (and once you've finished your drinks, dinner or the time seems appropriate,...whatever), ask her if she wants you to take her home and do exactly as she requests. End the night on a positive note by **not** going *nuts*,...at least in front of your ex!

Obviously, if the answer is "yes" and she wants to work towards reconciling the marriage,...give her a small kiss, have a celebration drink and enjoy the rest of the evening. Then put all your efforts into orchestrating a happy reunion and new relationship,...**largely on her terms**. There may still be much to do before you actually get back together. Don't resort to old habits along the way. Embrace the new 'you.'

In summary, if her answer is "no" and she wants to stay separated (and/or wants a divorce),.....**MOVE ON IMMEDIATELY** and don't look back. Don't wait for her under **ANY** circumstances. If she is to have a change of heart at a later date, you'll be the first to know! And, you'll still have an opportunity to consider it then. **But, don't wait**. Don't mope and don't waste energy on regret. Think of the whole thing as a learning experience for something and someone much better ahead! In fact, consider yourself lucky that you are a rejuvenated, upgraded man and remain confident that there will be another lady soon, because there will be for sure. As you are now a *new and improved* person, your opportunities will be far better in the future than they were in the past! Yet hers may well remain much the same!

WHAT TO DO IF YOU CHEATED

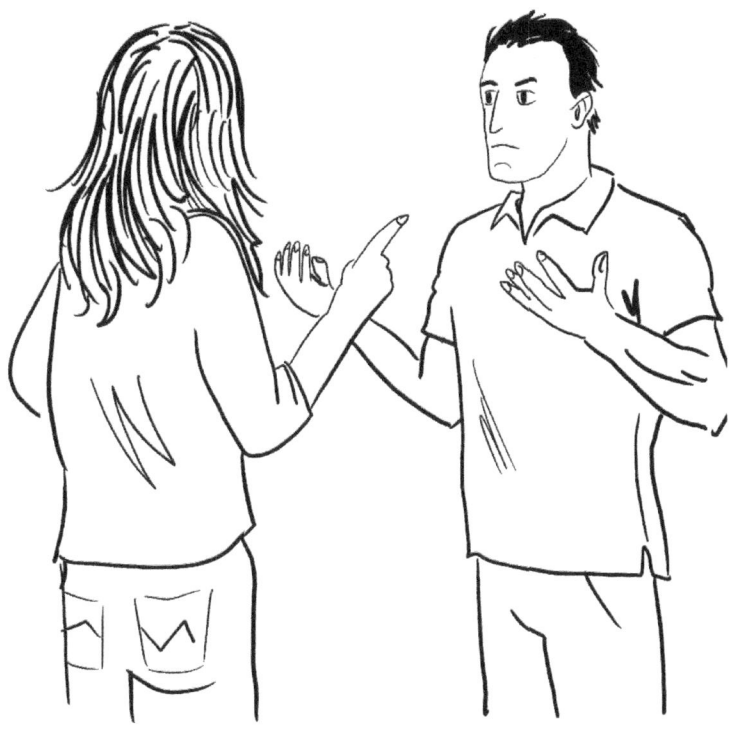

The road to reconciliation following a separation caused by an affair is no different than a separation caused by any other reason or reasons. In fact, affairs are rarely the only issue in a faltering marriage. So, if you genuinely do want your ex-wife back, the path is virtually the same (but with some additional items on your "To Do" list). On the presumption that you have read this whole book thus far, it is assumed that you have embraced and mastered all of its guidance and it is assumed that you have genuinely upgraded yourself. Then, should you get the opportunity to have that first post separation *real* interaction (as detailed under SPEECH item D above), you will be obligated to express your genuine regrets and make apologies related to your infidelity. Thereafter, and provided your ex-wife remains (at least somewhat) open to the possibility of working towards the restoration of your relationship, you might still have quite a lot to do to win her back completely. But, if you did get that positive acknowledgement from her, the ultimate goal of full reconciliation is very real and very attainable. You simply need to add a few things to your *itinerary*. In addition to all the other recommendations contained thus far in this book, you will need to regain the lost trust and actually demonstrate a sincere and total recommitment to your wife and the marriage. Here are a number of extra things that you can do to facilitate that. The following items 1 to 12 should be both brought into the first real interaction (SPEECH items A to D, discussed in the previous section) and implemented into your regular routine after a successful reconciliation.

1) Apologize profusely and repeatedly for both the repugnant act and for hurting your wife so severely. Tell her that the thought of losing her is *killing* you.

2) Make sure that you tell your wife that you stopped seeing the other woman (a long time ago) and you were never, ever in love with her! Be prepared to tell your wife exactly when (you broke off the affair) and I hope for your sake, that the termination occurred the day after your wife found out or sooner!

3) COME CLEAN entirely. That's right,...it's FULL CONFESSION time whenever she wants to talk about it. **You** screwed up,...so *fess up* and it had better be sincere. But, it's also a time to repent. Tell her what happened (**without sexual details**), tell her why it happened (**without blaming your wife**) and apologize profusely. For example,...."*This girl, who cuts my hair suggested that we go for a drink. I was stressed over some health issues and I didn't want to stress you out as well. I had a little too much to drink and before I knew it we were in bed. But, it's over and I'm really sorry. I know that I deceived you and broke the trust between us. I can't tell you how much I regret it. I'll do whatever it takes to fix this. I'll never see her again. I'll change my number so that she can't contact me,...whatever you want.*" And, that will be

What To Do If You Cheated

just the beginning of your apologies and concessions. You must be completely forthcoming but, NOT to the extent of providing sexual details. Chances are that if you cross that line, the reality of reconciliation will be drastically reduced! She doesn't need to visualize you *bumping and grinding* with Suzy Cute for the next 20 years,....not, at least, if you ever expect to have sensual relations again with your spouse.

4) Be truthful and remorseful and try to answer all her questions honestly. Your story must be truthful and **consistent** each time you tell part or all of it. Remember, you were caught lying and you don't want to get caught again!

5) As I mentioned earlier, take full responsibility even if you feel that she might have had some culpability. Clearly there were problems in the marriage. But, you betrayed your wife. So, "suck it up" and accept all the consequences. The fact that she might have contributed to your being unhappy and or unsatisfied in the marriage is no justification for betrayal. You can deal with your marital issues separately and hopefully under the guidance of a good marriage counselor. For now, you must fully accept and be completely accountable for your actions.

6) Do whatever your wife asks so that she knows that the affair is over. Moving forward, volunteer to share Facebook access, text messages and E-mail passwords with her.

7) Fully commit to saving the marriage. Tell your wife that you are prepared to do most anything for her and the union and do so. She needs to see the actions and results not merely hear the words of a liar! To that end, try to reconnect with her. The first step is communication. Talk to her more frequently throughout the day if you are back together and, at minimum, once every day if you are still separated. Ask how she's doing.

8) Volunteer to be accountable every minute of every day

especially if you have rejoined under the same roof. When you leave, tell her exactly where you are going and when you will be back. Effectively you must *punch a clock* for the foreseeable future. What's more you should cancel all your solo male activities. You should only be out of sight while at work. And, never be late (without calling with a perfectly legitimate explanation). Your wife needs to regain trust in you and, your being completely accountable, is the only way to do that.

9) Bring your wife little gifts frequently and apologize for your behavior and the pain that you caused each time you give her the present.

10) Be empathetic to your wife's feelings and be patient regarding her recovery. She will likely be on an emotional roller coaster ride for sure and as the result,...so will you! At the beginning it will seem like an unwinnable, uphill battle. She may even revert to "hating" you for a period of time. At minimum you have destroyed her image of you, she is still in great pain and you caused it. She is emotionally devastated, confused and hurt. So, stand by as necessary to support her. When she is feeling down, tell her again that you're sorry for hurting her. If she has more (or the same) questions about the affair,...answer them truthfully. Ensure that you do NOT change any part of the story. It is critical that the story remains consistent,...and so too regarding the "why it happened" explanation that you provide. Try to be resilient to any of her outbursts that might seem unreasonable. Reacting improperly will only make the situation worse.

11) Ask your wife for forgiveness,...frequently. Opportune moments are after you've done something nice for her and she is smiling. But, that should not be the only time that you ask for forgiveness. In addition, do something nice for her regularly.

12) If your wife is in agreement, seek marital counseling

immediately. If she is not in agreement, ask her again after a short period of time (possibly a few weeks). Therapy is highly recommended in these situations because there are undoubtedly other underlying marital issues and this will be an opportunity to address them. In addition, ask your wife if she would like to see someone on her own. Use professionals that have been highly recommended and who are substantially accredited. Ensure that they are also married! However, your wife should have the ultimate choice as to who you see.

13) Arrange regular and fun outings,...ones that your wife will enjoy. The idea is to return to a *couple's* path.

14) Demonstrate affection and appreciation for your wife every day. Call her mid-day and ask how she is doing.

15) While ongoing communication and open dialogue is important to establishing a new bond and connection,...make sure that you listen as well. Not always will she even want a response. When she does wish one,.. ask how you might help her to feel better!

16) Under no circumstances should you initiate sexual relations unless your wife asks (and she won't for a while) or unless your marriage therapist suggests such (and eventually, that professional will hopefully guide you both back to a normalized relationship that includes sex).

As I mentioned at the outset, less than 1 in 3 marriages will break up following an affair. However, it is rarely the affair itself that causes the separation. Frequently, it's the inability of the offending spouse (you, in this case) to properly confess, be remorseful and be truly empathetic to your wife's feelings. It will take time for sure and there will be many moments where the path will seem impossible to follow. She might test your loyalty to confirm your revived dedication. Or, she might get revenge by indulging in her own affair. There will be times that you feel that the pain, damage and upheaval is so great that it could never allow a return to normalcy and a reasonable relationship.

However, if she's indicated her willingness to trying to repair things, I urge you to have faith and "stay the course." Many devastated marriages have returned from the brink to a happy and intimate bond.

BRIEF SUMMARY OF THE ROAD TO WINNING HER BACK

1) Embrace the NO CONTACT and COOLING down period for 4 to 8 months.

2) Make appropriate financial preparations for your ex-wife and children (preferably on your own initiative and without a court order).

3) Spend as much time as possible with your children. Do not estrange yourself from them. They will neither understand nor forgive you.

4) Take the time to recuperate from your loss. You need to recover and it doesn't happen overnight. Rebuild your self-esteem and confidence by undertaking a new hobby, dating and engaging friends and family. Divert your attention away from your loss and get on with your life as there is no guarantee that you will get back together with your ex.

5) Learn some tried and true dating tips.

6) Take stock of all your failings and screw-ups. Make a list of your shortcomings and character flaws with particular emphasis on those that were instrumental in causing the separation. Include all the things with which your ex-wife expressed displeasure. Rectify as many of these unacceptable traits as possible.

7) Undertake and complete a personal makeover both emotionally and physically.

8) Stop worrying about the passing of time after the separation. Maintain the NO CONTACT rule for 4 minimum. It will work to your benefit as time and distance make the heart grow stronger!

9) Orchestrate a few *chance* encounters and stage the *coming out* of the new and improved *you*.

10) If the 3 to 4 brief encounters go without incident and your wife is no longer demonstrating any malice or displeasure with you,...it is time to ask her to meet (for dinner). More importantly, it is time to properly say you're sorry!

11) Meet with your ex and admit your mistakes, flaws and responsibility for the marriage breakdown. Apologize, show evidence of change and ask her to consider steps towards reconciliation.

12) Review the extra things to do if you were caught cheating! (See the previous section)

With luck, you are now almost back in the *saddle* with your ex and hopefully, that is where you want to be.

I've used this approach to reconciliation twice and it worked both times. Others I know have also tried it with good success. Interestingly, in one of my reconciliations, I did not receive a "yes" answer on the night of the first real interaction. It came a little later! And, by the time the reconciliation phone call did come from my ex-spouse, I was already comfortable in a new relationship with another lady and had no desire to have my ex-wife back! That was clearly one of the **benefits** of dating.

SO, CAN I EXPECT TO MOVE BACK IN TOGETHER TOMORROW?

Not necessarily, but likely soon. If your wife did agree to take steps towards reconciliation, I would doubt very much that she intends to turn over keys to the *house* just yet! She wants to be assured (by you) that you truly have changed and rectified the failings that prompted the separation. So, assuming that she wants to get back together, the next steps go something like this.

1) Stop dating any and all other women.

2) It's all about communication now. You are past the no contact rule. It's time to regularly text, call and send pigeons with warm endearing notes if necessary. Your messages should be sincere, heartfelt and genuine. ***Now's the time to communicate, communicate and communicate some more!***

3) Regularly ask your wife out on dates. Make sure that they are interesting and fun **for her**. Follow the dating tips referenced earlier in the book and do things that you didn't do before. ***Create a new routine***.

4) **Start a new hobby** *together* in which you regularly participate. Cooking, art classes, wine tasting, archery, horseback riding, bowling, a new language course are all good possibilities.

5) ***Be affectionate***. But, leave heavy romance (and particularly sex) out of the equation unless she initiates it or a counselor provides "rules of engagement." In other words, do not make any unsolicited advances in these regards. And, **don't be caught looking at other women!**

6) ***Suggest counseling***, and if she is amiable seek a reliable recommendation from friends and begin weekly sessions as soon as you have found the appropriate therapist. If the

therapist is a good one, he/she will give you both relationship building exercises to undertake. **While you want a therapist that comes highly recommended (by someone you both trust), the ultimate choice should be given to your wife!**

7) **Don't forget to keep the new 'you' apparent and visible at all times.** Continue practicing until the improvements become second nature. And, continue to look *sharp* each time you see your wife.

8) **Under no circumstances should you initiate a dispute, argument or disagreement.**

9) After a few weeks, ask your wife if she has stopped dating. Tell her that you have already done so. If she declines to do so, give her another few weeks and ask again. If she declines a second time inquire as to why. If her response is not perfectly reasonable, reconsider your desire to reconcile.

10) **Initiate family dinners** with your wife and children and make sure that you attend them (on time).

11) Communicate with your wife during each day to see how her day is going. **Be supportive of her stresses and needs.**

12) Ensure that every interaction and **every get together is completely stress-free**.

13) **Bring flowers** or a small present on date night and tell her that you love her.

14) Offer to do some of **her** chores.

15) **Always remain forthcoming and honest**.

16) **Try to 'be there' for your wife** whenever possible and tell her

that you are!

More than likely, your wife will ask you to reunite under the same roof within a few weeks. However, should that not happen, wait one month and then ask her when she might be interested in actually getting back together. Unless her response is ridiculously unacceptable (and I doubt that it will be), abide by her wishes. I expect that she will say something between *now* and a few months.

If (in the unlikely event) she expresses a time frame beyond six months and you believe it to be excessive, do not challenge or comment as to her requirements. Simply take the time to reconsider your options wherein you might make a different decision. Maybe, the reconciliation is not meant to be after all? Possibly one or both of you really don't want to reunite. There is no law that says that **YOU** can't change your mind. Possibly you might even wish to resume dating others. I do urge discretion if, you still wish to reconcile but also choose to begin dating again! That might be a recipe for disaster on both ends.

If you have followed the guidance in this book and reconciled with your wife, I expect and hope that you are both happier and stronger as a couple. However, the long term success of your relationship depends upon your ongoing efforts and not falling back into old ways and bad habits. Accordingly, continue to follow the above recommendations even after you resume cohabiting with your wife. In addition, don't forget the information delineated in Part 1 and particularly, "Why Women Fall Out Of Love." Keep up the positive efforts. Don't relapse, retain the new and improved 'you' and enjoy your *new* life with your *old* wife!

MAYBE YOUR MARRIAGE REALLY IS OVER OR SHOULD NEVER HAVE BEGUN!

Sometimes spouses are completely unaware that they are just not meant to be together. Other times, it becomes obvious to couples that their differences are far greater and/or numerous than they originally appreciated. Differences in cultural backgrounds, general views, politics, religion, child rearing, goals, morals, work ethics, finances and sex all contribute to marital disparity. Any one of these can easily disrupt a marriage and cause a deep divide. If more than one are present and parties are entrenched, then there is a need for serious reflection about parting ways.

Here are some simple signs that might suggest that you are better off going in separate directions.

1) You feel that it's over in your gut even though admitting it and acting on it might be very difficult and/or painful to one, the other or both of you. Maintaining the status quo is generally the easier path, but, often, not the correct path!

2) Your spouse's infidelity or substance abuse (of booze or drugs) continues unabated.

3) Your marriage is full of tension, secrets, distrust and/or disrespect. Arguments are not uncommon. Communication is limited and superficial and you avoid many sensitive topics. Possibly one or both of you have had, want to have or are currently having an affair.

4) There is no longer any emotional connection and/or support (of consequence) between you. One or both parties are indifferent towards the other.

5) There has been an obvious collapse of the relationship wherein the union no longer breeds happiness, comfort, solidarity or any

6) sense of companionship. Being in one another's company is not a pleasant experience.

7) There is limited or no physical connection. Kissing is forced and matronly. Sexual activity is often difficult (to perform) and/or not enjoyable. There is considerable individual social activity by one or both parties (without the other). One or both look for alternatives to going home.

8) There are serious unresolved issues or there are a multitude of lesser issues that similarly go unresolved. These issues continue to arise and lead to arguments.

9) You are genuinely happier when you are not at home and/or in the company of others.

10) You've done a soul bearing analysis of the pros and cons for remaining together (one that includes all of your faults as well as hers) and the *staying together* column comes up considerably short.

11) You or your spouse exhibit obvious signs of disinterest, lack of empathy, distance and little interest in supporting each other or the relationship.

12) Inappropriate behavior by one or both parents is causing undue stress, consequential mental anguish and/or general emotional harm to your children.

It is sad when a marriage dissolves. But, it is sadder when individuals remain together amid huge emotional strain, constant tension and complete unhappiness! I certainly don't suggest that breaking up is necessarily the better course of action or an easier path to follow,...especially if children are involved. But, realistically it might be better (for all) than remaining inside a toxic or unhappy environment. Certainly within a dysfunctional marriage, at least one of the spouses is despondent and, likely both are miserable. If a relationship has broken down in multiple key areas and if one partner genuinely believes it to be unrepairable, particularly if counseling was implemented and unsuccessful, then the realistic direction should be towards separation. Most likely in highly disparaging relationships, the dissolving of the marriage is ultimately positive for both spouses even if one party is not necessarily in agreement at the time of separation.

I was involved in two unhealthy, tension filled and highly strained marriages. Both wives were substance abusers. But, I never had the *balls* to pull the plug on either! Insecurity and *mini-me* ruled my life. But, boy was I happy when I was finally able to move on!

QUIZ – DO I REALLY WANT TO GET BACK TOGETHER WITH MY EX?

Before you take this quiz, please ensure that you have, at minimum, read this book in its entirety or the results will be skewed and totally unreliable. And, do NOT take this Quiz immediately after separation. Give yourself some time to heal or, once again, the results will be completely unpredictable and any drawn conclusions baseless. *It is preferable, for best results, if you have (already) read the book thoroughly, been separated for at least 3 to 4 months and implemented the lion's share of Steps 1 to 3 in Part Two of the book.* At that point, the Quiz will have its highest value.

I know that, at the best of times, men hate following instructions. We believe that we don't need instructions to put that BBQ together or assemble that bicycle! Nor do we need instructions to build that model with our kids! We are way too smart for all those things. Well, as you might recall, those endeavors didn't always work out quite the way our egos might have liked. So, please heed the aforementioned recommendation and follow the instructions suggested above. Taking this quiz prematurely will cause the results to be skewed and unreliable.

If, on the other hand, you completed everything to a "T" and are ready to be enlightened on the merits of getting back together with your ex-spouse, then take the following 50 question Quiz. Answer each question with only **one** check mark.

1. **How much baggage do you really have? In other words, did your ex think that you were high *maintenance*?**
   HIGH ____, MODERATE ____ or LOW ____

2. **How much baggage does your ex have? What level of *maintenance* is she?**
   HIGH ____, MODERATE ____ or LOW ____

3. **How much did you depend on your ex during the marriage? Were you more dependent on her than she on you?**
   NO _____, MODERATELY _____ or YES _____

4. **Have you enjoyed dating others during your separation?**
   NO _____, MODERATELY _____ or YES _____

5. **Did your ex-wife get along with your family?**
   NO _____, MODERATELY _____ or YES _____

6. **Did you get along with her family?**
   NO _____, MODERATELY _____ or YES _____

7. **Did your ex have a realistic and balanced view of the family financial status before the separation?**
   NO _____, MODERATELY _____ or YES _____

8. **Are your religious, ethnic, cultural and dietary preferences more similar or different to those of your ex?**
   MOSTLY DIFFERENT _____, SOME ARE SIMILAR _____ or MOST ARE SIMILAR _____

9. **Did your wife change substantially during the marriage due to menopause or any other factors?** YES _____, MODERATELY _____ or NO _____

10. **Was your wife unfaithful during the marriage?**
    YES _____, MAYBE _____ or NO _____

11. **Were you unfaithful AND was your ex-wife aware of your infidelity?**
    YES _____, MAYBE _____ or NO _____

12. **Prior to your separation were you somewhat ambivalent and complacent with the relationship or truly in love with your ex?**

COMPLACENT ____, SOMEWHAT COMPLACENT BUT IN LOVE ____ or IN LOVE ____

13. **If you asked your close friends and trusted relatives AND they were to answer honestly, would the majority believe that getting back together with your ex is a good idea?**
NO ____, MAYBE ____ or YES ____

14. **Do you honestly believe that your ex is still somewhat in love with you or, would she consider divorce a better option?**
NO ____, MODERATELY ____ or YES ____

15. **If you get back together, will there remain more than one major (and recurring) issue that you believe will never be resolved? Such major unresolved issues might include or pertain to any of the following and be specific to either spouse; drugs/alcohol, unemployment, hygiene/cleanliness, smoking, jealousy, emotional instability, flirting, money/finances, children, family interference, cultural differences, career, preoccupation with personal activities, etc.**
YES ____, MAYBE ____ or NO ____

16. **Do you and your ex have similar political views?**
NO ____, LARGELY ____ or YES ____

17. **Are both of you in similar physical shape?**
NO ____, LARGELY ____ or YES ____

18. **Is one of you more of a *home-body* while the other enjoys socializing?**
YES ____, SOMEWHAT ____ or NO ____

19. **In your opinion, did your ex enjoy sex with you or did she fake it?** NOT VERY MUCH ____, I THINK SO ____ or YES ____

20. **Did you enjoy having sex with your ex-wife?**
    NOT VERY MUCH _____, SOMETIMES _____ or MOST OF THE TIME _____

21. **Do you believe that your goals for the future are still aligned with those of your ex?** NOT VERY MUCH _____, I THINK SO _____ or YES _____

22. **Have your communication skills improved since your separation?** NOT VERY MUCH _____, I THINK SO _____ or YES _____

23. **Should you get back together, will the marital responsibilities be distributed between you in the same amount/way that they were before?**
    YES _____, SOMEWHAT _____ or NO _____

24. **When were you most in tune with the needs of your ex?**
    THE DAY YOU WERE MARRIED _____, THE DAY YOU SEPARATED _____ or TODAY _____

25. **Prior to separating, did you ever feel constrained in the marriage? In other words, did you feel that the marriage came with too many rules, dos and don'ts?**
    YES _____, SOMEWHAT _____ or NO _____

26. **At what point in your relationship would you say that you had the highest level of compassion and understanding for your spouse?**
    WHEN YOU WERE DATING _____, WHEN YOU GOT MARRIED _____ or TODAY _____

27. **Do you think that your ex has the "Grass is Greener" syndrome?**
    YES _____, SOMEWHAT _____ or NO _____

28. **Have you received any comments or compliments (from anyone) since your separation suggesting that you have changed (for the better)?**
    NO _____, ONE _____ or MORE THAN ONE _____

29. **How many new hobbies are you currently participating in?**
    None _____, ONE _____ or TWO or MORE _____

30. **How many different women did you date since your separation?**
    NONE _____, 1 - 3 _____ or 4 or MORE _____

31. **Have you sought counseling (since separation) for your issues?**
    NO _____, SORT OF _____ or YES _____

32. **How many counseling sessions have you attended?**
    NONE _____ 4 - 9 _____ or 10 or MORE _____

33. **How often do you drink alcohol or take drugs?**
    MORE THAN ONCE PER WEEK _____, ONCE PER WEEK _____ or RARELY _____

34. **How often did your ex drink alcohol or take drugs?**
    MORE THAN ONCE PER WEEK _____, ONCE PER WEEK _____ or RARELY _____

35. **When you took 'stock' and truly analyzed yourself, how many character flaws, shortcomings and/or behavioral issues did you identify in yourself?**
    NONE _____, ONE _____ or SEVERAL _____

36. **How many character flaws, shortcomings and/or behavioral issues did you improve or eliminate?**
    NONE _____, ONE/TWO _____ or MORE THAN TWO _____

37. **In your opinion, do you look the same today as you did when**

you were together with your ex?
YES _____, WORSE _____ or BETTER _____

38. **What aspect of your physical persona did you most improve since your separation?**
WARDROBE _____, CLEANLINESS/HYGIENE _____ or WEIGHT LOSS _____

39. **Do you smoke regularly?**
YES _____, OCCASIONALLY _____ or NO _____

40. **Have your social skills changed since your separation?**
NO _____, NOT SURE _____ or YES _____

41. **Do you think more about the good times that you had (when together) with your ex or the bad times?**
GOOD _____, EQUAL _____ or BAD _____

42. **Do you live in the past?**
YES _____, A TAD _____ or NO _____

43. **Were you a better person before you met your ex?**
YES _____, SOMEWHAT _____ or NO _____

44. **How lengthy would the list of your compromises be if you got back together with your ex?**
LENGTHY _____, MODERATE _____ or FEW _____

45. **Are you lonely from time to time?**
YES _____, SOMETIMES _____ or NO _____

46. **How do you feel about your ex's dating during your separation?**
I THOUGHT I WAS LOSING HER _____, JEALOUS _____ or FAIR GAME _____

47. **Is it possible that there is or might be someone out there that is better suited to you?**
    YES _____, MAYBE _____ or NO _____

48. **How would you rate yourself?**
    INSECURE _____, MODERATELY SECURE _____ or VERY SECURE _____

49. **Whose happiness is MOST important to you today?**
    YOUR EX-WIFE _____, BOTH PARTNERS _____ or YOU

50. **Do you like the *idea* of marriage (and a relationship) more than your actual ex?**
    YES _____, APPROXIMATELY THE SAME AMOUNT _____ or NO _____

Read the Conclusion (on the next page) to reveal your Quiz results.

CONCLUSION - BE CAREFUL WHAT YOU WISH FOR!

Well,...you got to the end of the book (and your journey) and hopefully in one (emotional) piece. And, you didn't die either! I sincerely hope that this book provided you with some enlightening and helpful inspiration. I also hope that you found the necessary guidance herein to implement many of the self-improvement suggestions. And, finally, I hope that you were able to reach your goals particularly if you remained unwavering in your desire to win your ex-wife back.

However, as you are probably aware by now, I left many hints throughout this book that you should be careful as to exactly what you wish for! Sometimes, what we think we want is not what we really need (or want) at all. Plus, in stressful situations, people tend to react hastily and always lean towards the apparent safety of maintaining the status quo. In this case, that would mean holding tight to any remaining marital strands that might exist when the separation first rears its ugly head. Yet, very often, our best course of action lies in the, as yet, unknown future and the road thereto. In fact, it is frequently the journey that provides the most benefits and not the ultimate preconceived goal.

So, with that in mind, I'd like to take this final opportunity to suggest that you reflect carefully on your path forward. A marriage is made up of two distinct people, neither of whom is perfect in any way, shape or form. In fact, human beings are so far from perfection that we require rules, laws and social pressures to keep us only *nominally* functional! Add to that the many spousal differences in backgrounds, ethics, aspirations and desires and you have a high likelihood of relationship failure.

Interestingly, I don't believe that achieving a successful marriage is more difficult today than in the past. People have not really changed appreciably in hundreds of years. Divorce rates are up substantially for sure, but, only because westernized laws have made it easier, the Church has been somewhat relegated to the fringes and it is no longer a *heinous* act. Just as many people probably wanted a separation and/or divorce two hundred years ago but, they were not readily attainable then. So, the unequivocal reality is that it is extremely difficult for couples in any generation to marry and remain happy and content with the same spouse until *death does us part*! But, for a marriage to be successful, I do believe that people need to be both similar and well matched with an absolute minimum of consequential differences that might lead to dispute.

Once again, I am not preaching that you abruptly *quit and run* if you aren't identical! I am simply (but strongly) suggesting that you take some time to ensure that this same woman is someone with whom you could actually go the distance,...and someone with whom you truly want to go the distance! Be sure that you will be comfortable with all of *her* annoying characteristics because I can pretty much guarantee that they will continue unabated into your future relationship!

Making any marriage work takes a great deal of effort. And, the effort should be reasonably equal on each side. In your situation, your ex will hold all the power as she left once and could threaten to do so again! So, if you honestly believe that you might have to initiate a vastly disproportionate amount of effort for which the rewards might be fewer and farther between, than maybe you should consider other options.

With luck, the above Quiz was helpful as well. If you checked the third box (the last box) for every question, your answers are the most supportive for you getting back together with your ex. However, if you checked mostly the first two boxes then I recommend that you seriously reconsider your desire to reconcile.

Hopefully, you truly embraced this book and particularly the section on taking 'stock' of your own misgivings and shortfalls. If you did and you actually rectified some of your failings, possibly your ex is not the woman who should reap those benefits. Once again, I am only suggesting reflection,...not running to the nearest exit with a "get out of jail" card!

But, consider again the failures and shortcomings of your ex-wife. Certainly, be fair, but, be thorough as well. Then ask yourself the simple question,....."Are the two of us a reasonable match?" "Do the similarities far outweigh the differences particularly surrounding the key elements of goals, ethics, children, finances and sex?" "Do I look forward to coming home at night?" "Does my wife present a minimum of frustrations for me?" If the answers to these questions are largely "yes",......I wish you and your spouse the absolute best that life can offer. May you both enjoy a long, happy and healthy marriage together.

One last thing, the contents of this book are, for the most part, an assortment of my opinions which, I consider to be quite credible. However, others might consider some or all of these opinions rather controversial. And, some might disagree vehemently. Even **you** might not share all of my views! So, use caution should you decide to discuss the book with your wife. On the other hand, if your spouse suggested that **you** read this book, pay close attention to the signals because her next *suggestion* may well be a separation!

Conclusion – Be Careful What You Wish For

GOOD LUCK

My next book will be entitled A Male's Guide To Becoming **THE BEST *LOVER* IN TOWN** and will be available soon. Learn how to please every woman in bed. Simple "tricks" for ordinary guys so that you can guarantee orgasms,.....theirs!

Made in the USA
Middletown, DE
09 January 2023

21718358R00096